CHERISHING GOD'S WORD

CHERISHING
GOD'S WORD

Mae Greenleaf

XULON PRESS

Xulon Press
2301 Lucien Way #415
Maitland, FL 32751
407.339.4217
www.xulonpress.com

Paperback ISBN-13: 978-1-6628-5812-3
Hard Cover ISBN-13: 978-1-6628-5813-0
Ebook ISBN-13: 978-1-6628-5814-7

Table of Contents by Topic

GOD'S WORD BRINGS HOPE, PROMISES AND CHANGED LIVES

Day 1: Kind Words

Daily Scripture Reading: 1 Thessalonians 1:1

Paul, Silas and Timothy, to the church of the Thessalonians in God the Father and the Lord Jesus Christ: Grace and peace to you. (verse 1)

ADENA* WAS DESPONDENT. THOUGH SHE HAS freedom in Christ, the restrictions placed on women in her Middle Eastern culture meant she could not even leave her house unaccompanied. The abuse and oppression weighed heavily on her heart. She felt like she had no voice.

When her brother learned about an opportunity to help narrate and record Bible stories in their language, he thought that might be just what Adena needed to lift her spirit. So the two packed up and made the long journey to a Bible translation center.

The cultures in this part of the world are largely oral, so recorded Bible stories are a wonderful, exciting way to reach people with the truths of the Scriptures. But after a few days of recording, it was clear that Adena still was depressed. A Wycliffe Associates team member asked her, "Have you considered that your voice recording these Bible stories could be what God uses to help someone know Jesus?"

Adena suddenly realized that God had opened the door for her voice finally to be heard—and to maybe help someone else see the light of His truth.

Her face lit up. With a renewed sense of purpose, she and her brother went on to record fifty Bible stories in their heart language.

Words of grace and peace—we need to hear and speak words that minister to our hearts and soothe the soul. Have your words invoked grace and peace to family, friends, and those around you?

Today's Prayer: Ask the Lord today to help your voice to speak grace, peace, and the message of salvation.

Name changed for security reasons.

Day 2: Be a Blessing

Daily Scripture Reading: 1 Thessalonians 1:3

We remember before our God and Father your work produced by faith, your labor prompted by love, and your endurance inspired by hope in our Lord Jesus Christ. (verse 3)

"If you asked me on Thursday noon of the second week if the goal would be reached, I would have had to say, 'I don't think so.' However, we serve a big and mighty God," reported Robert at the end of an awe-inspiring Bible translation training workshop in Southeast Asia.

One language group of thirty-five local people gathered, representing twenty-three churches and eleven different denominations. The goal was huge: to translate and type the entire New Testament in two weeks.

The thirty-five people were divided into groups. The hard work began at a good pace. Then came the difficulties: people got sick, several didn't arrive, one was called back to the village, two were called back to work, and more. The enemy worked hard to halt the translation of God's Word.

A large display chart was created with boxes to check off all the books and chapters completed. By Thursday night of the next week at nine o'clock, all the boxes were checked. The New Testament translation was complete.

So, the coordinators made a decision. Having brought along a mini Print On Demand™ system, they spent all night

Thursday printing, collating, and stapling almost 25,000 pages of Scripture! By Friday noon, each of the thirty-five translators held in their hands a copy of the New Testament, the first in their language, to take home to their villages. They had poured themselves out for this purpose.

You, too, know people who have poured themselves out to minister to you. Today you have the opportunity to praise the Lord for them.

Today's Prayer: Ask the Lord to show you how to minister to those who endure hardship for the sake of the gospel. Ask the Lord to make you a blessing to them today.

**Print On Demand is a high-speed, digital printing system that prints as many or as few real copies of God's Word quickly, literally "on demand."

Day 3: Pray for Lost Seniors

Daily Scripture Reading: 1 Thessalonians 1:8–10
They tell how you turned to God from idols to serve the living and true God. (verse 9)

Growing up in a small village in Cameroon, Jean Claude was immersed in superstition and dark rituals that were passed down for generations. Some involved animal sacrifices and even human skulls. As a boy, he would help his grandfather with the rituals and believed in their power.

"I really believed those things," Jean Claude said. "I believed in the skulls. I believed in their power—that the skulls could protect."

But that all changed when the Book of Jonah was translated into Jean Claude's heart language of Yemba. Reading the Scriptures in his own language turned his life upside down—and his father's, too. The two men turned their hearts over to Jesus. Soon after, Jean Claude's older sister also accepted Jesus into her heart. In their family of nine, three were followers of Christ, and generations of dark traditions were broken.

"My father died at almost sixty-eight years but as a Christian," Jean Claude said. "I thought to myself that surely there are many more Yemba like my father who are of the same mindset. And if I translate the Word of God and read it to many other people who are in their sixties like my father, then their lives could be changed just like my father's was. And that's what pushed me into Bible translation."

As you read your Bible, take time to think about senior citizens. Do you know someone who needs to hear about Jesus's love, forgiveness for sins, and salvation? Do you feel Jean Claude's drive to witness to them before it's too late?

Today's Prayer: Pray for the seniors whom you know do not follow Christ. Ask God to help you share the Good News with someone today.

Day 4: Pray for Your Enemies

Daily Scripture Reading: 1 Thessalonians 2:1–14

And we also thank God continually because, when you received the word of God, which you heard from us, you accepted it not as a human word, but as it actually is, the word of God, which is indeed at work in you who believe. . . . You suffered from your own people the same things those churches suffered from the Jews who killed the Lord Jesus. (verses 13–15)

A MIN* LIVES IN THE MIDDLE EAST, IN ONE OF THE most dangerous, most volatile places in the world to be a Christian. He has survived multiple assassination attempts since turning to Christ and becoming a Bible translator and church leader. But this time, it appeared that his attackers surely would succeed.

Three men armed with lead pipes and rods meant business. In a flash they unleashed a furious beating meant to kill. As their weapons delivered blow after blow, Amin was not filled with hate for his attackers. Instead, he was heartbroken by the fact that these men were lost and without Jesus. So as they beat him with metal pipes, he began praying aloud and urging them to turn from their sin toward Jesus. Imagine that! With the shadow of death looming over him, Amin was inviting his would-be assassins to experience a life of freedom in Christ.

God intervened. One dropped his pipe and fled. The other two, with tears in their eyes, dropped their weapons, dropped to their knees, and began pleading with Amin to tell them about Jesus.

Our Scripture passage today teaches that we are not exempt from suffering. You may not face a beating with lead pipes, but you may feel the sting of hurtful words.

Today's Prayer: Pray for and share God's love with the one who has hurt you.

Name changed for security reasons.

Day 5: Praying for Our Youth

Daily Scripture Reading: 1 Thessalonians 3:7

Therefore, brothers and sisters, in all our distress and persecution we were encouraged about you because of your faith. (verse 7)

"I F YOU JUMP, YOU WILL BE ACCEPTED," BERKI'S mother told him. "But if you refuse, you are no longer part of us."

In his heart Berki knew the ritual was not pleasing to God, and he stood firm. "I can't," he told his mother. "You can kill me, but I won't jump."

Referred to as "bull jumping," the ceremony begins with village women publicly gathering with bare backs, chanting, and blowing horns. Their goal? To provoke young men into whipping them with birch sticks. Their scarred backs would be seen as symbols of devotion to their pagan gods.

Each boy is then forced to run naked toward a line of bulls positioned side by side. Vaulting himself, he is to run across their backs to the other side. If he succeeds, he claims a bride (or several) and the right to father children and own cattle. Falling brings shame and humiliation.

Berki's family tried to kill him for his refusal. But God had other plans. A partner church of Wycliffe Associates recruited Berki to attend a Bible translation workshop, where he learned to share Bible stories in the local language. Berki is now an evangelist, riding his bicycle from village to village and proclaiming God's love.

This rite of passage, at first glimpse, may seem extreme. But think about what your culture expects of youth. Every young person who chooses to follow Jesus faces tough situations. Will you tell a young person in your church that you are encouraged by his or her faith? Your kind words may be just what he or she needs to remain steadfast.

Today's Prayer: Please pray for our youth who are experiencing pressure to conform to cultural norms and expectations rather than the truth of the gospel—especially those in your circle of influence.

Day 6: Open My Eyes, Lord

Daily Scripture Reading: 1 Thessalonians 3:8

For now we really live, since you are standing firm in the Lord. (verse 8)

"LET'S SEE WHAT THE BIBLE HAS TO SAY," THE pastor said to Sati.* Sati was a college student in South Asia at the time, but the pastor's words pierced his heart and have stuck with him ever since.

"The pastor satisfied me, not by his own argument, knowledge, or status, but with the verses of the Bible," Sati recalls. "I started studying the Bible . . . that was the turning point in my life. I believed and started following Jesus."

Even when persecution began, Sati held firm to his faith, clinging to the truths of the Scriptures. "Within six months of my baptism, my father was bitten by a very poisonous snake," Sati said. "He died. People were blaming me, saying that it was because I became a Christian. But I ignored them and continued to follow Jesus."

Today, Sati uses his Bible knowledge to help teams of his people translate Scripture so that others can "see what the Bible has to say." Recently, with the support of Wycliffe Associates partners, he helped complete the Gospel of Luke in the local language and distributed it to local churches. The response has been tremendous.

"My people are idol worshipers," Sati said. "But our Christian community is increasing day by day. We now have six house churches."

When facing difficult situations, consider opening the Bible to see what God has to say. When we study the Bible and use its principles, we can hold firm to our faith.

Today's Prayer: Ask the Lord to open your eyes to what He is saying to you as you read and study your Bible today.

Name changed for security reasons.

Day 7: Love More and More

Daily Scripture Reading: 1 Thessalonians 3:12–13

May the Lord make your love increase and overflow for each other and for everyone else, just as ours does for you. (verse 12)

"WE DON'T TREAT WIDOWS WELL AT ALL!" ONE pastor exclaimed, as others nodded in agreement. The group of pastors was testing the translation of the Book of Ruth as part of a language project in Southeast Asia. As Ruth's story unfolded in their own language, it pierced their hearts.

"When a man dies in our community, it's not unusual for his brothers to steal the widow's land and send her and her children to her parents' house with nothing," the pastor continued. "We need to start teaching people to help widows. We need men like Boaz!"

Through the translation of the Book of Ruth, a cultural shift is happening in the region as families and communities are learning how to treat one another with newfound respect and love.

One of the most exciting things about Bible translation is seeing people respond to the Scriptures in their own language and make life changes—like learning to love and respect one another. Paul encourages the new believers in Thessalonica to love one another more and more.

When you read the Scriptures, do you let God's Word change your life? How do you express love to your family members? To your friends? To your church family? Do you tell them that you love them, like Paul does?

Today's Prayer: Pray for someone today and then endeavor to express love for that person in a meaningful way. And say it!

Day 8: Living for Jesus

Daily Scripture Reading: 1 Thessalonians 4:11–12

Make it your ambition to lead a quiet life: You should mind your own business and work with your hands, just as we told you, so that your daily life may win the respect of outsiders and so that you will not be dependent on anybody. (verses 11–12)

DJABOU, A FORMER CHIEF AND HIGH PRIEST, WAS summoned by the big chief in the area. "You are our most respected high priest," said the chief. "If you become a Christian, who will lead us in sacrificing to the gods?" The chief warned Djabou not to become a Christian.

But Djabou felt nothing could stop him from following Jesus Christ.

Living in the far north of Cameroon, he and all the villagers struggle just to have food and water. Djabou makes and sells ropes for tying animals.

Today he attends a small church in his neighborhood. He loves Jesus. And he listens to his audio Bible in his own language and shares the love of Jesus with all who come by. He is a man on fire for the Lord.

Djabou sets the example for us today. Once a respected pagan leader who now makes ropes for the animals, he has been transformed from leading worship of the local gods to being in love with the Almighty God.

Take time today to think about your life. Does Jesus shine through your life, your work, and your words?

Today's Prayer: Ask the Lord today if you are living life the way He wants you to live. If not, pray that He will lead you in the changes He wants you to make.

Day 9: We Do Not Grieve As Those with No Hope

Daily Scripture Reading: 1 Thessalonians 4:13-15

Brothers and sisters, we do not want you to be uninformed about those who sleep in death, so that you do not grieve like the rest of mankind, who have no hope. (verse 13)

MEMBERS OF A LITTLE CHURCH IN THE MOUNTAINS of Southeast Asia prepared for a burial—a Christian burial, just as Boba Meli* had requested.

Ramahati Kiradi* and her husband had arrived four years prior and planted the church. The work was difficult. The area was home to many members of the Brahman caste—Hindu fundamentalists.

Boba Meli met the Lord Jesus through the ministry of Ramahati and her husband. Even though no one else in her family were Christians, Boba, the eldest member of this little church, wanted a Christian burial.

In preparation for her burial, they sang hymns and prayed together. There was praise in the air because they knew Boba Meli was with Jesus.

As believers in the Lord Jesus Christ, we have hope. We know that Jesus died and rose again. At death we will be present with Jesus. Hallelujah!

Does that bring a smile to your face? Just think—we will meet again those who have gone before us, loving Jesus. Take time today to think about your loved ones who are now with Jesus. Aren't you glad for the time you had with each one?

Today's Prayer: Praise the Lord today for the Christian heritage left by our loved ones who are no longer here. Thank Him for His gift of salvation so that we do not grieve as those with no hope.

Names changed for security reasons.

Day 10: Pray for Your Enemies

Daily Scripture Reading 1 Thessalonians 5:14–15

And we urge you, brothers and sisters, warn those who are idle and disruptive, encourage the disheartened, help the weak, be patient with everyone. Make sure that nobody pays back wrong for wrong, but always strive to do what is good for each other and for everyone else. (verses 14–15)

THE MWANGHAVUL PEOPLE IN NIGERIA NOW HAVE an audio version of the New Testament in their language. Because literacy is not common in their community, they listen to God's Word in groups and in their homes.

One woman said that before she started listening to the Bible in her home, her "husband was wayward." But she and her children listened together, and little by little her husband came to join them. As he listened to the Word of God in their language, his life was transformed. "He was no longer wayward," his wife said.

Whether we read or listen to God's Word, when we study the Bible daily, we learn God's instructions for living. We are challenged by His words: "Warn those who are idle and disruptive, encourage the disheartened, help the weak, be patient with everyone" (1 Thessalonians 5:14). We learn and are convicted to "always strive to do good for each other and for everyone else" (verse 15).

And like those among the Mwanghavul people, we, too, can be transformed when we listen to His words.

Today's Prayer: Ask the Lord to help you to not merely listen but to obey—to put into daily action His words of instruction.

Day 11: God's Will for You

Daily Scripture Reading: 1 Thessalonians 5:16–18

Rejoice always, pray continually, give thanks in all circumstances; for this is God's will for you in Christ Jesus. (verses 16-18)

GABRIELLE* IS IN CONSTANT DANGER OF IMPRISON-ment and isolation from family, because she is a follower of Jesus Christ and an active member of an underground church.

A few years ago she was arrested and jailed. Over her several-year imprisonment, she was interrogated, kept in solitary confinement, and brutally tortured. When finally released and asked about her horrible ordeal, she replied, "It was a honeymoon with Jesus." Through it all, God's love was poured into her heart—she enjoyed the presence of God.

Right now national believers living in horribly difficult places are hiding and translating Scripture into dozens of languages of the Middle East. And they want to reach out to dozens more language groups to help them translate the Scriptures into their languages—while they can.

Day by day, every hour they can, they work on Bible translation. The words of Scripture mean everything to them. They are committed—totally—to Bible translation and the cause of Christ.

We can almost see Gabrielle sitting in prison, much like Paul, singing, praying, and giving thanks for God's presence right there in her tiny cell. We know, too, that these persecuted national Bible translators rejoice as they see God's words in their language. They pray much and give thanks for such an awesome opportunity.

Today and every day we have the opportunity to live in God's will: to pray, to give thanks for all the Lord has done, and to rejoice in His presence with us in every situation.

Today's Prayer: Ask the Lord to remind you to pray and give thanks in all circumstances, even in suffering. Pray that you will feel His presence with you today.

Name changed for security reasons.

Day 12: Seeking the Truth

Daily Scripture Reading: 1 Thessalonians 5:19–22

Do not quench the Spirit. Do not treat prophecies with contempt but test them all; hold on to what is good, reject every kind of evil. (verses 19-22)

HE WAS CALLED "POISON MAN" IN HIS VILLAGE. For years Kiung was regularly called upon to use his poison on others. But under that shroud of darkness, he could not find the answers he sought for life and contentment. So Kiung began dabbling in "religion."

"I tried to do all of the good things," Kiung said. "I did everything the church told me to do. I followed all the laws, because I believed if I did enough of these things, I would get eternal life."

It wasn't until Kiung heard a teaching of God's Word in Patpatar, his heart language, that his life truly changed. "I began to realize that all of my prior ways and beliefs about the spirit world, the rules and traditions of the church, . . . they were not in line with God," he said. "Now I know that salvation is only by the work of Jesus. He died and rose again. I believe in Him."

Today Kiung is a pastor. He teaches and shepherds others who, like him, are seeking the one true God. And he has a message for Christians in the United States: "There is a huge need for the truth. We have churches. We've had them for a long time. However, they are not preaching the truth." They didn't have God's Word in their heart language.

Paul tells the Thessalonians to test everything. He says to hold on to the good—the truth of Jesus Christ. We hear many voices claiming to be the truth—do you test them by God's Word?

Today's Prayer: Ask the Lord Jesus to show you Himself—the way, the truth, and the life. Pray for discernment from the Holy Spirit so that you will know truth from error and have His strength to reject evil.

Day 13: Be Sanctified

Daily Scripture Reading: 1 Thessalonians 5:23–24

May God himself, the God of peace, sanctify you through and through. May your whole spirit, soul and body be kept blameless at the coming of our Lord Jesus Christ. The one who calls you is faithful, and he will do it. (verses 23–24)

"WHEN I SAW THE NEED OF THE PEOPLE—THERE are more than eighty languages in Ethiopia, and only eight have the [whole] Bible! . . . I saw that this is very timely and crucial work," said Dereje of Wycliffe Ethiopia. "When [the Bible] is in their mother tongue, they can understand it, they can love it."

In his younger years Dereje had attended a Bible study and accepted Christ. That foundation prepared him for when, in years of political oppression, he refused a job with the occupation government and was sent to prison. Despite the difficult experience, His heart belonged to the Lord.

Dereje shared his faith with fellow prisoners and even purchased a Bible in order to read to them in his mother tongue of Amharic. Today's verse was Dereje's sustaining verse in prison. Reading these words in Amharic, he realized that those who speak a different language would not understand God's Word in Amharic with the same depth and love. Reading, hearing, and studying the Bible in our mother tongues deepens our openness to the Lord God sanctifying us—to save us from sin and set us apart for His work.

Remember those who do not have the Bible in their heart language. Pray for them and support the national translators like Dereje. Consider this: Do you take time to study God's Word and His gift of sanctification? Think about finding a Bible study group that will encourage you.

Today's Prayer: Ask the Lord today to meet you as you read His Word, and pray that He will do a work in your life that will set you apart for what He has called you to do.

Day 14: The Presence of the Holy Spirit Brings Unity

Daily Scripture Reading: John 17:20–26

I have given them the glory that you gave me, that they may be one as we are one—I in them and you in me—so that they may be brought to complete unity. (verses 22–23)

NOT LONG AGO, COLLABORATION IN BIBLE TRANS-lation between churches in Nigeria was difficult with so many denominations. Collaboration seemed impossible with so many different ideas about how to translate the Bible. In fact, it felt like the Evil One had accomplished his goal in Nigeria—to divide the church.

Working with a translation partner in Nigeria, Wycliffe Associates scheduled a Bible translation workshop. Translation leaders, facilitators, and information technology personnel arrived on location to train and equip those who would gather to learn a new translation method.

Over 100 participants—church leaders from numerous denominations—all gathered at the workshop to translate the Bible. Even the state governor, who is a follower of Christ, sent a representative! The Nigerian church was ready to work together.

"I've never seen this many denominational leaders together at one place, at one time," said a participating pastor. The best part? The Holy Spirit clearly was present in this workshop!

Everyone worked together, united for a common goal. They want to see the Scriptures translated into their country's 230 languages.

We praise God that dozens of New Testaments have been completed! But many, many more Nigerian language communities still wait for God's Word to be translated into their heart language.

Today's Prayer: Dear Jesus, I pray my heart is open to the work of the Holy Spirit to help bring unity in my church so that we can serve You and Your work in the world. Amen.

Day 15: "I was made for this!"

Daily Scripture Reading: Psalm 33:1–5

For the word of the LORD is right and true; he is faithful in all he does. (verse 4)

THE FOLLOWING MESSAGE WAS RECEIVED FROM Rasa,* who is serving in South Asia:

"I was raised in a so-called Christian family. Praying was an option. Going to church or Sunday school was a choice. I made my own choice to know the Lord and attend church. It was the only place where I felt loved, knowing that someone had suffered and died for me.

"I was mocked and ridiculed by my own family and people I knew. And I was constantly reminded that I was (good for nothing). It became clear to me that the world needs to know God—to know the complete story of God, the New Testament and the Old Testament.

"When I received an email asking me to be part of a Bible translation event because I know the Hindi language well and have had theological training, I said yes. They needed me to interpret for the Wycliffe Associates team during a teaching session, so I volunteered. After we finished the training, my soul was so light, and my heart was filled with joy.

"All my life I have been thrown away and tossed aside like garbage. Little did I know that God was preparing me to participate not only in this one workshop but in many more to come. I know I was born to do exactly this work. I was made for this!"

Today's Prayer: Thank You, Father, for how You faithfully prepared Rasa for the work of Bible translation. Thank You for Your love and faithful preparation in my life so I can be used for Your purpose. Amen.

*Name changed for security reasons.

Day 16: The Power of God's Word

Daily Scripture Reading: 1 Peter 1:10–12

It was revealed to them that they were not serving themselves but you, when they spoke of the things that have now been told you by those who have preached the gospel to you by the Holy Spirit sent from heaven. (verse 12)

DANYAL* FROZE. THE MAN STANDING BEFORE HIM opened his jacket so Danyal could see the bomb. "I'm here to take your life for your belief in Jesus and for selling books that lead others to follow Him!" the man declared.

For a split second, Danyal couldn't think. Then he softly asked the man to read the framed words from 1 Corinthians hanging on the wall of his little shop: "Love is patient, love is kind. . . . Love does not delight in evil but rejoices with the truth." When the man finished, he closed his jacket and hurriedly left the shop.

A few days later, the same man walked into the shop. But he looked different. He told Danyal that he met Jesus the day he came into the shop with the bomb. This time he asked for a Bible. He wanted to follow Jesus Christ.

Recently, a four-week Bible translation workshop was held in this volatile region of the world. Attendees from the area, ranging from ages 15 to 60, translated the entire New Testament into Uu,* the local language.

The Holy Spirit works powerfully when people hear the words of Scripture in their own heart language. The Scriptures change lives—even the life of a would-be bomber standing that day in Danyal's small bookshop.

Today's Prayer: Dear Lord Jesus, I pray that the Scriptures I read today will be used by the Holy Spirit to work a change in my life, too. In Jesus's name. Amen.

Name changed for security reasons.

Day 17: But It Was Difficult to Greet Each Other

Daily Scripture Reading: 1 Peter 1:13–16

But just as he who called you is holy, so be holy in all you do; for it is written: "Be holy, because I am holy." (verses 15-16)

IN THE SPRING OF 2017, A LARGE BIBLE TRANSLATION training workshop was held in Bunia, Democratic Republic of the Congo (DRC) to train Bible translation teams from five language communities. All the teams would be translating the first Scripture in their people's language.

The local believers in Bunia were watching these soon-to-be Bible translators as they gathered. Since 1996, when the Rwandan genocide spilled into the DRC, these five language groups had found it difficult to shake hands or even greet each other, let alone work and eat together! We can only imagine the pain and loss each one has experienced in the recent past.

Following the workshop, Pastor Athanase wrote, "Greetings from Bunia. I would like to thank you so much for your prayers. We saw the hands of God upon us during our activities, and all things went as God wanted."

At the beginning, it was difficult for them to sit together or sleep in the same room. But during the two weeks of training, many were surprised. They were amazed to see these five tribes come together and have joy, fellowship, and unity of purpose—a testimony to God's power!

The Holy Spirit had set these men and women apart and brought them together to celebrate His Word in their respective languages. The word *holy* in Scripture means "to be set-apart" for God's work in the world.

Today's Prayer: Dear Lord, thank you for choosing these people to be set apart for Your work—to translate Your Word into their heart languages. Please prepare my heart to do the work You choose for me. In Jesus's name. Amen.

Day 18: Thrilled to Be Part of the Body of Christ

Daily Scripture Reading: 1 Peter 1:21–22

Now that you have purified yourselves by obeying the truth so that you have sincere love for each other, love one another deeply, from the heart. (verse 22)

THE BN* PEOPLE OF SOUTHEAST ASIA GREATLY respected Budi.* Some even feared him. In their culture, he was known as a powerful "dukun"—a witch doctor. Wherever Budi went, he carried a mighty dagger that was believed to hold powers for healing, protection, and a host of other things. Everyone knew he was not to be trifled with.

What they didn't know was that Bible translation was coming to their part of the world, and with it, a force more powerful than any Budi had ever known: the Holy Spirit. National translators came from all over the region to help, and when Budi read Scripture in the Bn* language for the first time, the Holy Spirit pierced his heart in a way he never knew possible. He's been a changed man ever since. "I've given up my 'powerful dagger' and replaced it with Christ," Budi said.

Today, Budi is thrilled to be part of the body of Christ and is actively helping to translate the New Testament into the Bn* language.

Praise God that others like Budi are coming to accept Christ too.

Today's Prayer: Lord Jesus, thank you for the purifying power of your truth for those who are far from you. Please help me to walk in obedience and to love all your people deeply. In Jesus's name. Amen.

Names changed for security reasons.

Day 19: "That is when I began to follow Jesus"

Daily Scripture Reading: 1 Peter 1:23–24

For you have been born again, not of perishable seed, but of imperishable, through the living and enduring word of God. (verse 23)

"ONE DAY I WALKED UP ON A MEDICAL CAMP IN MY neighborhood," M* began. "A man handed out medicine and checked for illness. Out of the corner of my eye, I saw a person reach under a blue tablecloth, pull out a Bible, and secretly hand it to my neighbor. I watched for an hour. He kept doing it—giving more Bibles away. Finally, I walked over. I kicked the table.

"All the Bibles scattered on the ground!" he continued. "Suddenly everyone knew what they were doing. There was an uproar, and the medical camp ended. Yet in the commotion, one of the leaders pulled me aside, spoke gently to me, and handed me a Bible. I don't know why I took it.

"Later, I read it in my room. The Old Testament was like what we were taught. But when I came to 'Jesus is the Son of God,' I threw that thing down! Of course, this business of Jesus as the Son of God is the dangerous stuff my teachers had warned me of!

"Some days later, I picked it up again. I saw Jesus say, 'Come to me, all who are heavy laden, and I will give you rest,' and 'Behold, I am with you always. Even to the end of the age.' "

M* stood smiling. "And that is when I began to follow Jesus," he said. "I began to preach. I met that medical man, and we became best friends. He mentored me. One day he was shot—and so I became the new mentor."

Today's Prayer: Oh, Lord, thank you for life everlasting that begins when we are born again! In Jesus's name, Amen.

Name changed for security reasons.

Day 20: An Eighty-Year-Old Translator

Daily Scripture Reading: 1 Peter 1:25–2:3

But the word of the Lord endures forever. And this is the word that was preached to you. (verse 25)

TEARS FILLED THE EYES OF EIGHTY-YEAR-OLD ANTSO* as he held in his hands the precious printed copy of the Gospel of Mark that he had just helped to translate into his mother tongue. This small portion of the New Testament is the first Scripture ever written in his own heart language.

Antso was one of eighteen mother-tongue translators from nine different language groups who traveled to a Bible translation training workshop in Madagascar. He was among the men who had traveled on foot for two weeks to catch the bus for the last leg of their journey, a ten-hour ride.

Antso may have been tired when he arrived, and the task ahead was difficult, but there was no stopping him when it meant that he would soon have Scripture in his heart language. He could hardly wait to get home with the Gospel of Mark in his hands so he could share the good news with his family.

The best part of getting God's Word into the language of every people? "The word of the Lord endures forever" (1 Peter 1:25). Antso is helping to provide the Scriptures for his children, grandchildren, and all the youth of his language community! His heart's desire is for them to read God's Word, learn of His great love and sacrifice, and experience His forgiveness.

Today's Prayer: Dear Lord Jesus, thank you for Antso's great love for Your Word and for his example of one empowered by Your Spirit. I pray that I, too, will follow the voice of Your Spirit and leave a legacy that honors Your name and carries Your Word to those who are far from You. I ask this in Jesus's wonderful name. Amen.

Name changed for security reasons.

Day 21: "Pray"

Daily Scripture Reading: 1 Peter 2:18–25

To this you were called, because Christ suffered for you, leaving you an example, that you should follow in his steps. (verse 21)

MOHAMMED* WAS SERIOUS. "PRAY FOR US," HE said. "The pressure is strong on those who follow Jesus. A friend reported to the Muslims that I am converting people. . . . They called me up. It was from my friend's cell phone. I went there, to his house. As soon as I walked in, six of them closed me inside, beat me with sticks and with bricks, and I fell. I am just one guy—what could I do?

"So of course, I went preaching again. And they came and said, 'Stop this. You must stop it. Leave this region, or you will die like your mentor.' But if I run away, who will tell the people about Jesus?

"Of course, I didn't stop. I cannot! They will kill me just like they killed my mentor and his mentor before him. They have told me so."

Mohammed was given the opportunity to stay in another city where ministry opportunities were less dangerous. But he would not stay.

"I must go back. I must. I cannot help it. Of course, they will kill me. But when I die, ten more will rise in my place."

We asked Mohammed, "What can we do for you?"

"Pray," he said.

Today's Prayer: Teach me, O Lord God, that the suffering of Your children is our call to prayer and service. Please prepare me, even now, to say yes to your Holy Spirit's promptings. Thank you, Jesus. Amen.

Name changed for security reasons.

Day 22: Look What God Has Done Already!

Daily Scripture Reading: 1 Peter 5:1–4

To the elders among you, . . . be shepherds of God's flock that is under your care, watching over them—not because you must, but because you are willing, as God wants you to be . . . being examples to the flock. (verses 1–3)

MARK IS RETIRED AND NOW HAS A SMALL SIDE-JOB helping others with their financial planning. When he reviewed his personal income at the end of the first quarter, he wrote two checks. The first check was for his tithe, and the second was for half of the balance of his income—a large amount that amazed even him!

Enclosed with the check that he sent to Wycliffe Associates, Mark noted, "At the Wycliffe Associates event I attended, I made a promise by faith far beyond my ability."

Mark was moved to share in Wycliffe Associates' ministry of Bible translation—the Church Owned Bible Translation strategy and goal to get a Bible translated into every language in the world.

"As I contemplated how I would ever accomplish [that faith promise]," he continued, "I made a commitment to the Lord: 'I will give to the kingdom half of everything I make this year in my financial practice.' Look what God has done already! This check represents half my income—and it's only the end of the first quarter!

"I am amazed but not surprised. The next few years will be incomprehensible to watch."

Mark's enthusiasm to share how God answered his prayer is a huge encouragement to those in his circle of influence—his flock, so to speak—to trust the Lord with their lives and their finances.

Today's Prayer: Dear Lord Jesus, please help me to have the courage to follow You. And make me an encouragement to those I love. Thank you, Jesus. Amen.

Day 23—"When I suffer, you will restore me"

Daily Scripture Reading: 1 Peter 5:10–11

And the God of all grace, who called you to his eternal glory in Christ, after you have suffered a little while, will himself restore you and make you strong, firm and steadfast. (verse 10)

"FOR SIX DAYS, I WAS IN POLICE CUSTODY," SAYS Pastor Ri,* who oversees a church in South Asia. His crime? He sheltered a group of orphans in his church for nine days while they were being connected with relatives.

Such persecution is becoming commonplace in Pastor Ri's homeland. The government's new constitution bans evangelism and conversion, and Christians who share the gospel openly are being jailed and even tortured.

"We have been praying to our Lord," Pastor Ri says. "If it is time to be persecuted according to His Word, we would like to accept it."

The translated Scriptures are needed in this part of the world. Believers in this region live hours away from the nearest church. They are separated by thick mountain ranges and treacherous terrain. They desperately need God's Word in their own language so they can turn to it for truth and assurance.

Two translation workshops were conducted for the Ni* language—Pastor Ri's heart language. Thirty mother tongue translators came together to begin translating the New Testament.

By the end of the first workshop, the team had finished eight books of the New Testament. By the end of the second training, translators had translated the entire New Testament. Copies then were printed using printers that Wycliffe Associates provided so the Scriptures could be distributed in the villages.

And yet, there are still thirty-five more language groups in their region without any translation of God's Word.

Today's Prayer: Lord Jesus, thank you for the promises in Your Word, like the verses I read today. When I suffer, you will restore me and make me able to stand strong. Thank you, Jesus. Amen.

Name changed for security reasons.

Day 24: When Walls Speak God's Word

Daily Scripture Reading: 2 Peter 2

The Lord knows how to rescue the godly from trials and to hold the unrighteous for punishment on the day of judgment. (verse 9)

NAOMI* WITNESSED THE POWER OF WORDS FIRST-hand in her early days as a student. Though she grew up in a devout Muslim family in a Muslim country, her parents sent her to a Christian missionary school so she could get a good education and learn English. Naomi recalled how the walls of the school were filled with Scripture verses. And the words found their way into her heart.

Years later when her husband abandoned her, Naomi spiraled into a very dark place. She searched desperately for answers and for God. She looked for God in the Koran. Nothing. She searched for Him in the shrines. He was not there. And when she sought advice from a "holy man," he told her to stand on one leg all night while chanting.

At her wit's end, Naomi recalled the words from her old classroom walls. She realized that she had never seen anything like the words of love and hope that were written there. About that time a friend invited Naomi to a prayer meeting.

When she heard the pastor share yet more powerful words from the Bible, she knew in her heart that this was the only real truth, and she committed her life to Christ.

Today, Pastor Naomi shares the power of God's Word with others. She recently attended a Bible translation training workshop, where she helped to translate Scripture into her native tongue, the Pi* language, which is spoken by more than one hundred million people.

Today's Prayer: Dear Lord Jesus, thank you that Your Holy Scripture is powerful to uphold us when we walk through suffering. Please help me to remember Your words of love and peace when I face trials. In Your precious name. Amen.

Names changed for security reasons.

Day 25: Unfamiliar Paths

Daily Scripture Reading: Isaiah 42:16

I will lead the blind by ways they have not known, along unfamiliar paths I will guide them; I will turn the darkness into light before them and make the rough places smooth. These are the things I will do; I will not forsake them. (verse 16)

WAYNE'S GOAL WAS TO LEARN TO DRIVE NAILS with his eyes closed. So he practiced diligently until he mastered the task—and then some. But there was a purpose behind Wayne's plan: he was going blind, and he decided the best thing he could do was to prepare for it.

At the time, Wayne owned some rental properties that needed renovating. So he went to work on the repairs, and as he did, he practiced driving nails and using tools as though he already could not see.

Today Wayne is completely blind. And he can hammer, frame, roof, and finish as well as any seeing carpenter.

As a Wycliffe Associates volunteer, Wayne has devoted his time and skills to construction projects around the world to accelerate the life-changing work of Bible translation.

For Wayne, it appears his blindness is a mere inconvenience in his commitment to serving God.

Maybe you're wondering how you could make a difference in God's kingdom with your abilities.

It has been said that God is not looking for our ability as much as our availability. Like Wayne, will you trust God to lead you along unfamiliar paths in your service to Him? There is no Guide more trustworthy.

Today's Prayer: Heavenly Father, I need your direction as I travel on the paths You have laid before me, whether familiar or unfamiliar. Please use me to bless someone today.

Day 26: Preaching without Words

Daily Scripture Reading: Acts 4:13

When they saw the courage of Peter and John and realized that they were unschooled, ordinary men, they were astonished and they took note that these men had been with Jesus. (verse 13)

"I HAVE NEVER KNOWN SUCH PEOPLE," MADELINE thought. "Why did they come so far to help strangers? What makes them so happy?"

Madeline had taken a housekeeping job for a Wycliffe Associates short-term volunteer team in Cameroon. The team had traveled to her country to bring practical help to Bible translators so they could focus their efforts primarily on the work of Bible translation.

One of the team members noticed Madeline was puzzled by their joy and kindness and asked a wise Christian woman who knew both French and English to speak with Madeline. The woman patiently listened to Madeline's questions and then explained God's great salvation through Jesus Christ.

The following Sunday, Madeline experienced that salvation for herself as she made the decision to receive Jesus as her Savior.

For team members Michael and Brenda, Madeline's life-changing decision was an answer to prayer. Long before they met Madeline, they had asked God to bless their trip to Cameroon in a very specific way.

"Lord God," they prayed, "equip us to reflect You in our actions, since we cannot use words." God used their godly behavior to transcend the language barrier and lead a young woman in a faraway land to Himself.

Your life is a silent testament to the gospel of Jesus Christ. You may not always have the opportunity to verbally share the Good News with unbelievers around you, but you can demonstrate God's love with your attitude and actions.

What will your conduct say today?

Today's Prayer: God, give me the wisdom and strength to daily live out the gospel before those who do not yet know Jesus Christ. May my silent witness be a positive and powerful one.

Day 27: Powered to Persevere

Daily Scripture Reading: 2 Corinthians 1:7

And our hope for you is firm because we know that just as you share in our sufferings, so also you share in our comfort. (verse 7)

MARCIA WENT TO CHAD, ONCE KNOWN AS THE poorest nation on earth, to help people learn to translate the Bible. Marcia was excited about her work and looked forward to her teaching assignment. Even her spacious classroom seemed perfect—that is, until she experienced the first of many power failures that would constantly disrupt her teaching.

During one particularly lengthy interruption in power, Marcia and her students moved their tables outside to continue their studies, using adapters to connect their computers to truck batteries. The constant disruptions began to test Marcia's enthusiasm, and she could see that it also was affecting her students' progress.

Then a Wycliffe Associates volunteer construction team arrived on the scene and built a new training facility, complete with running water and electricity. Marcia is grateful for what the team of volunteers did to help her, her students, and the other Bible translators. "Now things are less adventurous," she says, "but much more satisfying!" Often we assume the important work of God's kingdom is being carried out by pastors and missionaries like Marcia. But meeting the practical needs of others can be crucial kingdom work as well. Whether it's taking part in a construction project, providing a meal, or running errands, the seemingly ordinary tasks of life can become extraordinary when dedicated to God's service.

What practical needs can you help meet today? When you step forward in faith to serve Him, you just may be surprised by the outcome.

Today's Prayer: Pray that God would open doors of opportunity for you to help meet the practical needs of a pastor, church staff member, or missionary you know. Ask God to show you how you can be a blessing to this person and his or her family.

Day 28: The Courage to Continue

Daily Scripture Reading: Philippians 3:14

I press on toward the goal to win the prize for which God has called me heavenward in Christ Jesus. (verse 14)

WHEN THE BIBLE TRANSLATORS LEARNED THEY had to leave Colombia because of security concerns, they wondered how they possibly could continue their work. Random acts of violence, displaced families, and killings were common news of the day.

First their support workers were asked to leave, and then they were asked to leave as well and to complete their work from outside Colombia. Of course, the translators longed to finish the work to which God had called them: translating the New Testament into the Epena language. "After we had adjusted to one new situation, it seemed like we were face-to-face with another obstacle that would make our work even harder to complete.

"We felt like the children of Israel under bondage to Pharaoh in Egypt, and we were being told by our taskmasters, 'Make the same quota of bricks, but now you will have to gather your own straw.'"

But through the generous support of Wycliffe Associates supporters who helped fund the Colombia Transition Project, these translators were able to complete their work. They even were able to return to Colombia twice yearly to work alongside their Epena co-translators.

Sometimes we face the greatest obstacles and the most overwhelming circumstances when we are in the will of God, carrying out the work He has called us to do. Are you facing a seemingly insurmountable task today? Don't give up! God can—and will—help you finish the work you have begun for Him.

Today's Prayer: Pray for God to strengthen your heart and give you the courage you need to face the circumstances that may be overwhelming you today.

Day 29: Compelled to Care

Daily Scripture Reading: 2 Corinthians 5:14

For Christ's love compels us, because we are convinced that one died for all, and therefore all died. (verse 14)

I N AN ISOLATED REGION OF A SOUTH ASIAN NATION, canyons cut deeply into the terrain, where, for centuries, people have carved out their lives on the unforgiving slopes.

But when a 7.6-magnitude earthquake rattled the region, it seemed as though their entire existence came crumbling down the mountain. Thousands upon thousands of lives were lost, and those who survived needed new homes, schools, hospitals, and offices. And, they needed to know they were not forgotten.

With the help of supporters and volunteers, Wycliffe Associates was able to answer God's call to reach out to the people of this devastated region and show them His love. A Wycliffe Associates volunteer team partnered with the local people to help rebuild their homes and lives—and help open their hearts and minds to the reality of God's love for them.

Volunteers later commented, "It was [a] moving experience . . . the people prayed for us. . . . They were so grateful for any help we could give them."

It has been said that people don't care how much you know until they know how much you care. Our acts of compassion can help open hearts to receive the good news of

Jesus Christ. It may be a coworker, family member, friend, or neighbor who needs to be reminded that someone cares.

Taking a few moments to reach out with an act of compassion can make all the difference in their world.

Today's Prayer: Lord, use me to show Your love to those in my life, and open doors for me to share the gospel with those who don't know You.

Day 30: Finding Joy in Service

Daily Scripture Reading: 1 Corinthians 15:58

Therefore, my dear brothers and sisters, stand firm. Let nothing move you. Always give yourselves fully to the work of the Lord, because you know that your labor in the Lord is not in vain. (verse 58)

WHEN A WYCLIFFE ASSOCIATES VOLUNTEER named Shirley accepted a tutoring assignment in Benin, little did she know what an impact her presence would have on the family—and what a difference her assignment would make in her own spiritual journey.

Before arriving in Benin, she was surprised to learn that she would be sharing a home with the children and their parents, Jim and Sandy. But then Jim suddenly became ill with a virulent strain of malaria and had to be evacuated to South Africa for medical treatment. Sandy accompanied him, while Shirley stayed behind to care for the children.

Having already lived in the home, Shirley could adapt more easily to her new role, which included overseeing the national helpers.

When Shirley began attending church with one of them, it quickly became the favorite part of her assignment. "The highlight of my time in Benin was my relationship with the people of the church," Shirley says. "Being part of a worshiping community, hearing the Word preached with fervor, and entering into prayer with the people of God was a blessing."

Almost a month passed before Jim was well enough to return home, and Shirley's help was just as important during his long recovery.

Sometimes God calls us to serve Him in surprising ways. But when we step forward to accept His unexpected assignments, not only will we be a blessing to others, but we will be blessed as well.

Today's Prayer: Ask God to help you be flexible in your service to Him. Pray for a willing heart that is ready to respond to the needs at hand.

Day 31: Loving the Unlovable

Daily Scripture Reading: Luke 6:35

But love your enemies, do good to them, and lend to them without expecting to get anything back. Then your reward will be great. (verse 35)

IN THE AFTERMATH OF A DEADLY EARTHQUAKE THAT shook her village in Indonesia, Mrs. D* bathed twenty-one bodies in preparation for their burial.

Mrs. D, her husband, and two children live in a village where they are the only Christians. So when tragedy struck, they took the opportunity to demonstrate God's love to their neighbors in a very unusual way.

According to Indonesian custom, the dead must be bathed prior to burial. "No one wanted to do it," Mrs. D recalls, "so I had to clean the bodies. . . . Not until after we finished did their friends and relatives come to help with the burial."

Even the local Muslim leader praised the Christians for their compassionate help. Mrs. D and her husband hope that one day, their friends and neighbors in the village will come to experience God's love firsthand through a relationship with Christ.

Wycliffe Associates also took the opportunity to express God's love to the people of Indonesia by offering construction expertise, as well as funding for humanitarian aid and rebuilding efforts.

It is not always easy to show kindness to someone who has treated us unfairly or who might not appreciate our efforts. Yet the Bible reminds us to "serve one another humbly in love. For the entire law is fulfilled in keeping this one command: 'Love your neighbor as yourself'" (Galatians 5:13–14).

Who needs your expression of God's love today?

Today's Prayer: Lord Jesus, please give me Your heart of compassion for those in my community who do not know You, and open my eyes to opportunities to show Your love to them.

Name changed for security reasons.

Day 32: Tragedy Turned to Triumph

Daily Scripture Reading: 2 Corinthians 12:10

That is why, for Christ's sake, I delight in weaknesses, in insults, in hardships, in persecutions, in difficulties. For when I am weak, then I am strong. (verse 10)

EXPERIENCING A CAR ACCIDENT AND A ROBBERY ALL in one trip would be enough to discourage most people from embarking on a similar journey in the future—but not Russ.

A construction superintendent for Wycliffe Associates in Papua New Guinea, Russ traveled to a remote village to upgrade the power supply for a Bible translator who lived and worked there. When Russ and his helping partner, Neil, had completed their work, they were the guests of honor at a dedication service celebrating the completion of the Gospel of Luke in the Nek language.

But the next day as they drove toward home, they hit a pothole in the road, rendering their vehicle inoperable and sending Russ and Neil to the hospital. To add insult to injury, some unscrupulous locals seized the opportunity to rob them of their possessions. Yet Russ remained unfazed by the turn of events. "As much as I felt the Lord's presence in the village," he recalls, "I felt His presence during the accident and robbery. . . .

"The pain of injury and loss could not be compared to the joy of God's presence. I look forward to the next village trip."

Has a hardship in your life taken away your joy? God is still at work, even in the most discouraging circumstances. As author Warren Wiersbe says, "We do not live on explanations; we live on promises." Will you trust God's promises today?

Today's Prayer: Pray for God to fill your heart with joy, regardless of your circumstances. Ask Him to help you discover new ways to bring joy to the lives of those around you.

Day 33: From Payback to Peace

Daily Scripture Reading: Colossians 3:13

Bear with each other and forgive one another if any of you has a grievance against someone. Forgive as the Lord forgave you. (verse 13)

"IT'S OKAY IF SOMEONE KILLS ME," SIVINI TOLD THE people in his village. "I have accepted Jesus now and am ready to die if He wants me to. I have confessed everything to God, so I am not afraid."

Sivini lives in Papua New Guinea, where his people, the Usarufa, had been at war with the Kamano in a seemingly endless cycle of bloodshed and retaliation. As a respected village leader, he had planned attacks against the Kamano people and had killed many of their men.

But now Sivini is a Christian and a co-translator, working to bring God's Word to his people—and to his former enemies.

So when men from his village wanted revenge against the Kamano for murdering one of their own, Sivini faced a dilemma. He called six of the men to accompany him to a meeting with the Kamano leaders, where he explained that his people did not want to fight—and they would not be retaliating. He went on to tell the Kamano elders that he had killed many of their men in the past, but God had changed his life.

Today, Sivini's people and the Kamano live in peace. And it all began with one heart transformed by the gospel.

The Bible tells us that "while we were still sinners, Christ died for us" (Romans 5:8). Although we don't deserve God's mercy, He has shown us mercy through His Son, Jesus Christ. Is there someone who needs your forgiveness and mercy today?

Today's Prayer: Ask God to bring to mind anyone who is in need of your forgiveness, and pray that He would give you a renewed heart and a willingness to forgive.

Day 34: Watch the Hurting Whom God Sends Your Way

Daily Scripture Reading: Ephesians 3:14–21

I pray that you, being rooted and established in love, may have power, together with all the Lord's holy people, to grasp how wide and long and high and deep is the love of Christ. (verses 17–18)

CALIXTE, WHO HAD GROWN UP IN A MUSLIM HOME, looked around to see who had called out. There was no one. Once more he gripped the doorknob of the church exit, desperate to return home and take his life. He already had purchased the pills. Calixte was allowed to use the church's instruments, and he wanted to play the guitar one last time before ending it all.

Again he heard the voice he would later come to understand as the Holy Spirit: "Don't go!" Calixte knew in his heart that he wasn't just hearing things. He looked around, but there was only a small prayer group huddled on the other side of the building.

That's when one of the Christians looked up, saw the puzzled look on Calixte's face, and quietly invited him to join them. As the group prayed for Calixte, he felt God's peace and love wash over him. And when they shared their own testimonies, he knew he wanted what they had. So, he prayed to receive Christ.

Calixte, now a pastor, works with our translation partner in Burkina Faso to train new Bible translators. Pastor Calixte speaks six languages, and through Wycliffe Associates Bible Translation training workshops, he has helped four language groups complete their translation of the New Testament in less than a year! Soon these language groups will have the entire Bible in their heart languages.

Today's Prayer: Dear Jesus, please help me share the gospel with someone who needs Your love and forgiveness. Show me those who are hurting, and help me notice those moments when You bring someone in my path to share Your love. Amen.

Day 35: Never Give Up

Daily Scripture Reading: Hebrews 12:1–3
Fixing our eyes on Jesus, the pioneer and perfecter of faith. For the joy set before him he endured the cross, scorning its shame, and sat down at the right hand of the throne of God. (verse 2)

Edy* RECENTLY PARTICIPATED IN A WYCLIFFE Associates Bible translation training workshop in Southeast Asia. Edy and his family lived about an hour away, but he left his small shop in his hometown for two weeks. He was a true inspiration to the team as they worked together translating the books of the New Testament.

During the second week of the translation training workshop, Edy was asked to give his testimony. He shared that within a very short time, three devastating incidents had befallen his family, wiping out their savings and everything he had worked so hard to establish. Under such circumstances, many people would have given in to the weight of the loss and questioned their faith. Not Edy.

In fact, Edy's faith is stronger than ever, and he is committed to translating the Bible in his mother tongue so that others can read about the saving grace of his Lord Jesus Christ.

Following his testimony, Edy sang this song: "God has a plan that is bigger than all the unthinkable. I will not give up on anything before I try all that I can. My heart surrenders to Your will, because I believe that God has a plan."

Edy was then asked how he was able to hold on to his faith during such trials. His response was simple and straight from the heart: "Nothing compares to what Jesus endured on the cross to save us."

Today's Prayer: Dear Heavenly Father, thank You for Your salvation. Please help me to never give up but to instead live out Your plan with endurance. I pray this in Jesus's name. Amen.

Name changed for security reasons.

Day 36: Bring Down the Walls

Daily Scripture Reading: John 17

Holy Father, protect them by the power of your name, the name you gave me, so that they may be one as we are one. (verse 11)

THE TENSION IN THE ROOM WAS THICK. DISTRUST, resentment, and hostility were rife among the Bible translators from five different tribes—people groups who have been at war with each other for years.

These translators from the Democratic Republic of the Congo had come together for a two-week Bible translation training workshop to begin translating the Bible into their own heart languages. But many of the attendees had serious doubts that this joint effort could ever work. After all, the pain and trauma they carried with them were remnants of the Rwandan genocide. They had experienced great suffering and loss, and blame rested on the other people in the room.

Could they shake hands? Share a meal together? Indeed, the emotional walls between them were tall and thick. This would take a miracle.

But God also was in the room, and He has a long track record of miracles. Slowly, as focus shifted to the work of Bible translation, the Holy Spirit began chipping away at hardened hearts. As His words were translated into their heart language, the translators from these warring people groups spoke to each other like never before. Barriers began to crack, then crumble, and ultimately shatter into oblivion.

Joy took over as the translators came together in Christian fellowship, unified by a common purpose: to translate God's Word and glorify Him!

Today's Prayer: Dear Father, may the Holy Spirit bring joy and peace to my soul. Show me the walls that divide my community, and guide us to reconciliation. May I be united with my brothers and sisters of the faith so that we may serve You. In Jesus's name. Amen.

Day 37: Serve by Faith

Daily Scripture Reading: 1 Peter 4:7–19

If you suffer as a Christian, do not be ashamed, but praise God that you bear that name. (verse 16)

"I USED TO BE AN AL-QAEDA FIGHTER," SARA* TOLD the church elder. "I had an AK-47, and I used to go fight with them and then nurse the injured as well."

Sara had been coming to the church for a couple of months, and she was always covered—obviously Sunni Muslim. When God ultimately took hold of her heart, she just had to tell someone.

"I started coming, and I heard the gospel and came to know Christ. I was afraid to tell you at first, because I was afraid you would report me."

Sara is not alone. Several Bible translators serving with us today were once terrorists and are living testimonies to the power of God's Word to bring someone from death to life. They are from the most volatile parts of the world—places where the Bible doesn't exist, places where it may appear that God doesn't exist. But He does!

Scriptures for New Frontiers is our strategy to advance Bible translation in high-risk areas that are hostile toward Christianity. Already national translators serve by faith in secret, secure locations, quietly working to translate forty different languages of the region. Wycliffe Associates helps to equip these courageous servants with tools and valuable resources, such as reliable internet connectivity, training, and Print On Demand** systems.

When we watch the news and see the violence, let's pray for believers diligently translating God's Word for their own people in these dangerous new frontiers.

Today's Prayer: Dear Jesus, thank you for giving eternal life to all who believe in You. I pray today for Bible translators in the New Frontiers who need Your protection as they share Your Word despite persecution. Help me to serve You by faith and without shame. Amen.

*Name changed for security reasons.

**Print On Demand a high-speed, digital printing system that prints as many or as few real copies of God's Word quickly, literally "on demand."

Day 38: "My lips have found laughter again!"

Daily Scripture Reading: Deuteronomy 31:6

"Be strong and courageous. Do not be afraid or terrified because of them, for the LORD your God goes with you; he will never leave you nor forsake you." (verse 6)

"I KNOW THAT EVEN THOUGH WE CAN'T GO OUTSIDE, I also know no one is looking for my father here," said Mary,* who is now in hiding. "I also don't hear my mother crying. My lips have found laughter again. Thank you, thank you, thank you!"

Young Mary was among a group of 22 local believers Wycliffe Associates helped rescue from a Middle Eastern country that was taken over by an anti-Christian regime. Jesus followers in this part of the world know persecution is an everyday reality. But seemingly overnight this network of small underground churches desperately needed to be evacuated. With the help of partners like you, they fled to a safe house we secured within the country. They then went to an airport where they prayed that God would prevent security from noticing the "non-Muslim" label on their ID cards.

Security never even asked to see their IDs! They boarded the plane to a safer country.

Jesus followers would much prefer to stay in their own country so they can share the gospel with their non-believing neighborss. We often work with underground church networks to train their people to become Bible translators, translating God's Word into their own mother tongue.

Today's Prayer: Loving God, Thank You for the successful evacuation of our brothers and sisters. I pray for their comfort and strength in You and that they can continue their translation work.

Names changes for security reasons.

Day 39: Be Equipped

Daily Scripture Reading: 2 Timothy 3:14–17

All Scripture is God-breathed and is useful for teaching, rebuking, correcting and training in righteousness, so that the servant of God may be thoroughly equipped for every good work. (verses 16–17)

AABID* HAD A DREAM. HE FOUND HIMSELF IN A BIG room, like a dormitory, with bunk beds lined up along the walls. As Aabid looked around the room, the beds turned to gravestones. But not his bed. He recognized a framed picture on the wall. It was one of the familiar pictures of Jesus Christ. Slowly, it came to life and beckoned Aabid to follow. "You need to leave this place."

Aabid had never had a dream like that. It touched him deeply. In response to the dream, he began to question the Muslim faith. Almost immediately, he was ostracized by his friends and family and even thrown in jail. No charges. No trial. Yet Aabid's nine months in jail became an unexpected blessing.

Every week a Christian brother visited the jail and taught Aabid about the life of Jesus Christ. After nine months of having been faithfully taught from the Word of God, Aabid was released.

Aabid, prepared in the faith, shared God's message and learned how to plant churches among Muslim communities. Once a Muslim imam, but now a Bible teacher, Aabid attended a conference where he trained a team of thirty-five men and women to sensitively engage Muslim communities with the gospel.

Today Aabid is one of the foremost church-planting trainers in southern Ethiopia. He says that he has trained close to four thousand men and women to share God's message and plant churches in their own language communities.

Today's Prayer: Dear Lord Jesus, please equip me today, through reading Your Word, to do the good work that You have planned for me to do. Amen.

Name changed for security reasons.

Day 40: God's Word Finds the Lost

Daily Scripture Reading: Luke 15:11–32

This brother of yours was dead and is alive again; he was lost and is found. (verse 32)

FAVEN* WAS HEARING SCRIPTURE IN HER OWN LANguage for the first time—the story of the prodigal son. As she listened, the words pierced her heart, and she knew this was truth. She also knew that she had to share these words with her husband, Haile.*

When Haile arrived home, Faven urged him to watch the video. He, too, was moved by God's Word in his native tongue, and together they placed their faith in Jesus Christ.

Faven and Haile are just two of the many new believers in Northeast Africa who desperately need your prayers. In this Muslim stronghold, they are at constant risk of severe persecution. Since the government has shut down the evangelical churches, Christians now meet secretly in homes and even in cemeteries to try to stay under the radar. If they are caught, they are rounded up like cattle and crammed into large shipping containers—makeshift prisons that are blazing hot during the day and frigid cold at night. It is heartbreaking.

Yet God's message of love and salvation through His translated Word can undo the evils being endured by Christians in this part of the world. That's why Wycliffe Associates is committed to Bible translation training for believers in the region. For the Ta* language group alone, believers have translated, printed, and distributed fifty Bible stories to people like Faven and Haile.

Today's Prayer: Dear Lord Jesus, this dear couple and many believers face unimaginable persecution simply for calling You "Lord." Please keep them safe when they gather to worship You. I pray they will know Your comforting presence in their midst. Help me to remember them in prayer so that more prodigals can read Your Word and come home to You. In Jesus's name. Amen.

Names changed for security reasons.

Day 41: "I'm so thirsty; I just want to know more."

Daily Scripture Reading: Philippians 4:1–9

And the peace of God, which transcends all understanding, will guard your hearts and your minds in Christ Jesus. (verse 7)

A s Bible translation continues around the world, the remaining language communities that still have no Scriptures are in the most difficult and dangerous countries—countries where extreme persecution of Christians and the constant threat of terrorism mean that all translation work must be kept under wraps. But don't confuse silence with inaction!

Abir* grew up in just such a hostile country under the teaching of Islam. As a young man, he began questioning his faith, dissatisfied with the Muslim religion. His heart, life, and community lacked peace. Then Abir happened upon a Christian program being broadcast on television. Intrigued, he contacted the station to learn more about this Jesus. He was put in contact with a man named Robert,* who agreed to meet with him.

In the weeks that followed, Abir and Robert studied the Scriptures that had been *translated into Abir's language*. He found answers to his many questions and began to sense truth in the Bible. Then one day, he looked up at Robert with tears filling his eyes and said, "I want to be a disciple of Jesus."

Today Abir continues to grow in his newfound faith. "This is so incredible," he says. "I am free. I have such peace inside me. I am so thirsty; I just want to know more."

Today's Prayer: Dear Jesus, thank You for the Scriptures that teach us about being Your disciple. Fill me with a thirst for Your Word and the peace that transcends all understanding. Lead me to put into practice what I learn from Scripture. In Jesus's name. Amen.

Names changed for security reasons.

Day 42: Bring Hope to the Hopeless

Daily Scripture Reading: Psalm 119:105–120

You are my refuge and my shield; I have put my hope in your word.
(verse 114)

IN NORTHWESTERN KENYA, A REFUGEE CAMP IS PER-
haps the last place on earth you would expect to find Bible
translation underway. Home to 185,000 refugees from
Ethiopia, Somalia, Sudan, and South Sudan, the camp has
been a place of sorrow.

Yet amid suffering and hopelessness, a blessing has taken
hold in the form of Bible translation. A Bible translation
training workshop was held for eleven Sudanese language
groups. Leading a Bible translation workshop in a refugee
camp, which includes taking bucket baths and sleeping in
rooms with no doors, is an extraordinary challenge. It was
difficult charging computer tablets and having no lights for
translation teams to work at night.

In the Refugee Camp, seventy-three new mother-tongue
translators attended the training. Each translated Scripture
into their own language. To date, this is the largest Bible translation training workshop ever held in Africa. And more refugees are taking notice.

"Sometimes when I see people carrying the Scriptures in
their languages, I feel frustration," says Hani.* "I ask myself,
'Why not me? Why not a Bible in my language?'" Hani is no

longer asking these questions. Hani and others are planning more Bible translation training workshops so they also can start Bible translation in their languages. Bringing the hope of Jesus Christ and His Word to the refugees truly is a miracle. Now the Camp is also a place of immense hope.

Today's Prayer: Heavenly Father, there are so many language communities in refugee camps who need to hear the gospel. Please help them get the Bible into their heart languages. Help me to be an instrument in Your hands to share Your hope with others. In Jesus's name. Amen.

Name changed for security reasons.

Day 43: Pray for the Persecuted Church

Daily Scripture Reading: Colossians 1:9–14

Blessed is the one who perseveres under trial because, having stood the test, that person will receive the crown of life that the Lord has promised to those who love him. (James 1:12)

A YOUNG PASTOR BECAME THE BIBLE TRANSLATION leader for his language group in a certain Muslim country. Then the first Bible translation workshop that had been planned was suddenly cancelled. The pastor was jailed because he was telling Muslims about Jesus. The government declared that he would spend two years in jail, but in ten days he could appeal the sentence.

So, the Wycliffe Associates Prayer Watch team, along with many others, began to pray. They prayed, watched, and waited for the appeal and the final ruling. The appeal was delayed, the team kept praying, and God answered. Finally, this young pastor who trusted in the power of God was released.

Pastors, Bible translators, and Christians living in Muslim and communist countries continue to be harassed, jailed, tortured, and even executed for teaching about Jesus, the Son of God. Continually they just ask us for prayer. Why? Because they know that God always answers prayer. Let's pray that persecuted believers will have wisdom, understanding, be fruit bearers, and grow in knowledge of God. Pray for their strength, endurance, and patience under trial. Pray for them to have God's Word in their languages. Then we all will give joyful thanks to the Father.

Today's Prayer: Dear Jesus, thank You for the freedoms I have to worship, study, and share Your love for all people. Please help me remember to pray for those who are being harassed and persecuted because they love and worship You. I pray that very soon, everyone will have access to the Bible, Your precious Word, in their heart language to help them persevere under trial. Thank You, Lord Jesus, for answering prayer. Amen.

Day 44: God Faithfully Provides

Daily Scripture Reading: Deuteronomy 15:4–11

Give generously to them and do so without a grudging heart; then because of this the LORD your God will bless you in all your work and in everything you put your hand to. (verse 10)

MARK ATTENDED A WYCLIFFE ASSOCIATES BANquet several years ago. At the close of the banquet, he made a faith promise—a financial commitment to the Lord—to help advance the work of Bible translation. At the time, Mark's home building business gave his family a very comfortable lifestyle. He left that banquet feeling confident that he could fulfill his commitment.

Shortly thereafter, an economic recession hit hard, especially in the housing market. Mark downsized to a smaller home, but he still couldn't send in his faith promise.

The thought kept nagging in the back of his mind—he must fulfill his faith promise commitment.

Mark then read a book about how God owns everything, including his business. As Mark thought about all he'd read, he believed the time was right. He made the decision, wrote a check for the full faith promise commitment, and in the midst of that act, his heart changed.

Before this experience, he gave only when he had extra money. He knows now that God wants him to give monthly the amount he had committed at that banquet. As Mark began to give each month, he realized that God was sending new customers his way. Now he has more work than he ever anticipated. God continues to bless Mark, his business, and Bible translation.

Today's Prayer: Dear Lord, thank You so much for Your faithfulness to me. When I think about people who do not have one verse of Scripture, they are indeed poor. Please teach me to give generously with a full heart, thankful that You are teaching me from Your Word. I pray this in the precious name of Jesus. Amen.

Day 45: "We believe in your Jesus!"

Daily Scripture Reading: John 5:16–30

Whoever hears my word and believes him who sent me has eternal life. (verse 24)

T HE EXCITEMENT WAS PALPABLE. A BIBLE TRANSLA-
tion workshop had finally come to this Southeast Asian
community, and the local church couldn't wait to begin. But
four Muslim men also had arrived at the workshop, which
immediately alarmed the lead trainer. He asked the church
leaders why they had invited them. The church leaders assured
him that they had prayed, and God told them to invite them
to the workshop.

The four Muslims were supervised by Dr. F,* a former
Baptist pastor and seminary president. They diligently
immersed themselves in the Word of God, and each day they
asked Dr. F about Jesus.

Being well schooled in the Scriptures, Dr. F could have
just rattled off the answers to his students' questions. But he
had a better idea. Instead, each day he assigned them specific
Bible verses to translate into their mother tongue—passages
that answered their questions.

One particular day, after translating the verses Dr. F gave
them, the four men came to him and said, "It is amazing! We
believe your Jesus!" God's Word in their heart language had

reached their souls with truth, love, and grace. At the end of the workshop, they asked Dr. F to baptize them.

For these Muslim men, reading the Bible in their mother tongue made the person of Jesus come alive to them. When we, too, immerse ourselves in Scripture, regularly reading and studying God's Word, it indeed will answer every question we have about who Jesus is and why He gave His life for us.

Today's Prayer: Dear Lord, help me to remember those who long to have the Bible in their mother tongue, so they can hear Your words and believe in Jesus. In Jesus's name. Amen.

Name changed for security reasons.

Day 46: A Test of Faith

Daily Scripture Reading: Isaiah 55:9

As the heavens are higher than the earth, so are my ways higher than your ways, and my thoughts than your thoughts. (verse 9)

A FEW DAYS AFTER CHRISTMAS, GLENN AND HIS family were hiking and picnicking when he received word that their home had been burned to the ground. After stealing computers and other valuables, vandals set fire to their home, destroying fifteen years of memories.

Glenn is a missionary pilot who lives with his family in Southeast Asia, where he supports Bible translation by transporting translators and supplies into the area. While Glenn could have become angry at God because of what happened to his family's home, he saw the circumstances in a new light.

Glenn had been studying the sovereignty of God and immediately thought of the words of Job: "Naked I came from my mother's womb, and naked I will depart. The LORD gave and the LORD has taken away; may the name of the LORD be praised" (Job 1:21).

"God is not sovereign in a vacuum," Glenn says. "He works within our hearts through His Word to make us know that He is sovereign." Glenn recognized that his involvement in the ministry of Bible translation helps make it possible for others to learn about God's sovereignty as well.

His family's home has been rebuilt by Wycliffe Associates volunteers, and Glenn continues his work as a pilot in support of Bible translation, with a new appreciation for the blessing of having God's Word in his language.

Maybe circumstances in your life have left you with questions—or perhaps even anger—over what has happened. Like Glenn, will you trust God's sovereign ways in your life? You may find one day that your tears have been turned to triumph.

Today's Prayer: Ask God to help you learn from the challenges you are facing right now and help you use them as opportunities to grow in wisdom and faith.

Day 47: In the Midst of a Miracle

Daily Scripture Reading: Psalm 66:16–20

God has surely listened and has heard my prayer. (verse 19)

WHEN MARGARET BEGAN HAVING HEART PROB-lems, she was told she was not well enough to continue serving on the mission field. She was heartbroken. But she knew that God had a plan.

Living in Australia, away from the mission field, Margaret was awakened one night by a vivid dream in which God told her to visit one of her tenants. Pastor Ako and his wife, Lily, were surprised to see an elderly woman standing in the doorway.

"A vision came to me at 2:00 a.m.," Margaret began. "The Lord showed me your face. He said, 'My son is in need. Walk over and see him.'" The Lord had instructed her to give Pastor Ako a savings card she'd had for years.

The three of them quickly realized they were in the midst of a miracle. Pastor Ako told Margaret he needed an operation for a serious heart defect. He then explained how he and Lily had been up praying until 2:00 a.m. that God somehow would provide. Margaret's savings card covered Pastor Ako's surgery, and he has since returned to Papua New Guinea, where he is helping lead Bible translation for thirty languages.

In a beautiful way, Margaret's desire to minister has come to pass. "My heart is at peace now," she told Pastor Ako. "You are taking part of me to Papua New Guinea to serve the people I love and long to serve."

Today's Prayer: Dear Father, thank You for reminding me that You hear my prayers and answer. Help me remember that Your timing is always perfect. In Jesus's name. Amen.

Day 48: They Were Thrown into Prison. Repeatedly!

Daily Scripture Reading: 2 Corinthians 12:5–10

That is why, for Christ's sake, I delight in weaknesses, in insults, in hardships, in persecutions, in difficulties. For when I am weak, then I am strong. (verse 10)

Firuz* and Lana* are a husband-and-wife team deeply committed to each other and to translating God's Word for their people. They live in a Middle Eastern country where Christians are persecuted. Because Firuz and Lana love to share the gospel, they have been arrested and thrown in prison. *Repeatedly.*

The couple's attorney kept wondering why these people were willing to be arrested and thrown in prison for their faith. He just had to know. Finally, he asked for a Bible to read so he could find out for himself.

Firuz and Lana have seen God work through many challenges as they reached out to others with the gospel. After Firuz's most recent arrest, he was in the prison library writing Scripture notes. The head guard asked to see what he was writing. He was so moved by what he read that he asked Firuz to teach these things to the other prisoners. Firuz had the privilege of sharing his Christian faith with nearly one thousand prisoners!

Even where there is persecution, people are reading God's Word in their heart language for the first time. Lives are being transformed. Believers like Firuz and Lana depend on the power of Jesus Christ for strength. And, they are determined not to let anything stand in the way of getting His translated Word into the hands of their people.

Today's Prayer: Dear Jesus, thank You for being our strength when days are difficult and we are weak. Amen.

Names changed for security reasons.

Day 49: God Knows Us, and He Loves Us

Daily Scripture Reading: Romans 8:31–39

For I am convinced that neither death nor life, neither angels nor demons, neither the present nor the future, nor any powers, neither height nor depth, nor anything else in all creation, will be able to separate us from the love of God that is in Christ Jesus our Lord. (verses 38–39)

Mos,* a Muslim living in a Muslim country, chose to follow Jesus when the Lord came to him in a dream and said, "I tell you that I am the Lord, and I am the one who leads you to the truth."

At first, God protected Mos and his wife from the daily persecution and violence. "With the help of the Holy Spirit, I started to preach the gospel, and six households accepted Jesus as their Savior," Mos said.

Due to more severe persecution, culminating in fire being set to his home, he and his wife relocated, and Mos again began teaching others about Jesus. Then twenty-eight more people accepted Christ.

One day as Mos was teaching about God's love and forgiveness, the people sincerely asked, "Does God know our language? Can He speak our language?" They only knew of God from a Bible in a different language. Mos replied, "Yes, God knows us, and He knows our language."

Today, Mos is a full-time minister of the gospel and a Bible translator. His team has translated the New Testament, and soon they'll have the entire Bible in their language.

Today's Prayer: Oh, Lord Jesus, how awesome that You led Mos to the truth, and now he leads others to You. As I learn more of the truth of Your love and forgiveness, please give me boldness to share it with others. Amen.

*Name changed for security reasons.

Day 50: Jesus's Sacrifice Was Enough

Daily Scripture Reading: Romans 3:21–26

God presented Christ as a sacrifice of atonement, through the shedding of his blood—to be received by faith. (verse 25)

NAI,* A GUARD AT THE TRANSLATION CENTER IN Cameroon, had received God's Word in His language, and it touched his heart. Almost daily, he was struggling to reconcile biblical truths with the traditions of his culture.

Again, Nai was called back to his village to offer a sacrifice of a rooster or a goat. This time his uncle's grave was caving in. His family believed it was a sign that his uncle's spirit was angry and that Nai must offer a sacrifice in "Kontri Fashion" to appease the spirit—or people would die.

Nai dug deeper into God's Word. The Holy Spirit began to open his eyes and his heart. That's when he approached a Bible translation team leader and asked, "Does it mean that if I really give my heart to Jesus, I don't need to go to the village and do Kontri Fashion (sacrifice) to the gods anymore . . . that Jesus is God's Kontri Fashion?"

Yes, Jesus's sacrifice on the cross was enough. That day, Nai decided to follow Jesus. No longer did he need the traditional religion of fear and bondage.

Today's Prayer: God, You are holy, and You have saved me, and Nai, through Jesus's perfect sacrifice. Thank You for giving Your Holy Spirit to help me understand Your words of love and salvation. In Jesus Christ's name I pray. Amen.

Name changed for security reasons.

Day 51: Pray that the Holy Spirit Will Intervene

Daily Scripture Reading: 1 Peter 5:6–11

Your enemy the devil prowls around like a roaring lion looking for someone to devour. Resist him, standing firm in the faith, because you know that the family of believers throughout the world is undergoing the same kind of sufferings. (verses 8–9)

EVELINE AND HER HUSBAND, A PASTOR AND NATIONAL Bible translator, opened their home to local believers for a time of fellowship, praise, and prayer. And that evening, extremists ambushed their home and brutally killed five people, including Eveline's husband.

Eveline suffered severe head injuries from a machete and had one of her hands severed. Her three children witnessed the horror unfold before their eyes. Healing would need to take place—physical, emotional, and spiritual. Partners like you quickly responded.

Because of the gifts to the Wycliffe Associates Emergency 911 Fund, we were able to cover Eveline's hospital bills, provide trauma counseling, and move her and her children to a safe location. She even started a small retail business, selling food items and basic household goods to provide for her family. It's a true example of the body of Christ in action.

Eveline's story provides a snapshot of the violence and persecution that has overtaken Cameroon. Sadly, this was once a peaceful country. The Enemy is doing everything possible to hinder Bible translation—but God's work continues.

Today's Prayer: Oh Lord God, please move in miraculous ways in Cameroon. Intervene on behalf of these precious people who need the hope found in Jesus Christ. And, Lord, please work in my heart so that when I see a neighbor in need, I'll be prepared to help. In Jesus's name. Amen.

Day 52: Help Me to Follow Your Truth

Daily Scripture Reading: Ephesians 1:15–23

For this reason, ever since I heard about your faith in the Lord Jesus and your love for all God's people, I have not stopped giving thanks for you, remembering you in my prayers. (verses 15–16)

"I WAS JUST A CHILD WHEN MY FAMILY ARRANGED MY marriage to a man whom I knew as my relative," Zili says. "I was so upset, I fled to a city."

Along the way, Zili met another girl who was fleeing a polygamous marriage arrangement. The girls turned to the authorities and were taken to a nearby mission school. There at the school, Zili was introduced to Jesus.

"There was a Bible study class in the school, and we used to have devotions," Zili says. "In 2001, I accepted Jesus as my Savior in the school devotions. Now I have committed my life to bring the Word of God to my people."

Today, Zili is a member of a team of Bible translators working to translate the New Testament into her heart language. In fact, Bible translators for thirteen different language groups in the region have participated in a Wycliffe Associates Bible translation workshop to translate the New Testament for their families, friends, and communities.

Today's Prayer: Dear Jesus, thank you for Zili's faith and desire to give her people God's Word. Thank you, too, for the people in my life whose faith and love for our church family inspires me. Help me, Lord, to not only follow their example but to also remember them in prayer. In Your name I pray. Amen.

Day 53: Jesus, a Light in the Darkness

Daily Scripture Reading: Matthew 5:10–16

Blessed are you when people insult you, persecute you and falsely say all kinds of evil against you because of me. Rejoice and be glad, because great is your reward in heaven, for in the same way they persecuted the prophets who were before you. (verses 11-12)

PATHAN* WAS A YOUNG MUSLIM WOMAN FROM A ruthless sect in the Middle East, where marriages are strictly arranged between Muslim families. Shane,* a follower of Jesus Christ, loved Pathan.

Knowing Pathan's family never would allow them to marry, the young couple ran away to a missionary organization for refuge. There Pathan accepted Christ and was baptized. Soon after, she and Shane were married.

The couple had a son and two daughters while they lived in hiding for ten years. But eventually, Pathan's parents located and contacted them. They assured Pathan that they really wanted to know their grandchildren.

Pathan's parents visited a few times. Then one day her father and brothers beat Shane severely and threw him out of his own home. Shane returned to find his beloved Pathan had been strangled to death. He was heartbroken. Her family had murdered her for the perceived shame she had brought upon them by abandoning their Muslim faith.

Believers face persecution in the Middle East every day. They need the translated Word of God to shine His light into a very dark and hopeless place.

Today's Prayer: Oh Lord, may our persecuted brothers and sisters be assured of Your presence, and may they soon have the Bible in their languages. And, Lord, may I be Your light in dark times. In Jesus's name. Amen.

Names changed for security reasons.

Day 54: Where Three or Four Are Gathered, There's Bible Translation!

Daily Scripture Reading: Ephesians 2:8–10

For it is by grace you have been saved, through faith—and this is not from yourselves, it is the gift of God—not by works, so that no one can boast. For we are God's handiwork, created in Christ Jesus to do good works, which God prepared in advance for us to do. (verses 8–10)

H E WAS A TERRORIST AND WREAKED HAVOC IN COM-
munities across the Middle East for many years—until he met Jesus Christ in a dream.

Dreams of Jesus have become growing occurrences in the Middle East. Though we can't tell you in which country he lives, we can tell you that Pastor A* is married now. He and his wife not only help shepherd believers in underground churches, but they also have participated in Bible translation workshops.

Pastor and Mrs. A helped translate the New Testament into an Arabic dialect. What's more, after the completion of each New Testament book, they use Bible Translation Recording Kits (BTRKs) to create audio recordings of the newly translated Scriptures for those who cannot read. Each translation team is provided a BTRK, which includes a computer tablet, translation and recording software, and a microphone.

While intense persecution of Christians in this region is a stark reality, Bible translation continues in small groups of three to four translators. The great news is they soon will have the New Testament in their languages!

Today's Prayer: Dear Lord Jesus, thank you for Pastor and Mrs. A's efforts to provide their people with audio versions of their Bible translation. Please, Lord, help me to seek out a need that I can fill so I can take part in my church's ministry. Amen.

Names changed for security reasons.

Day 55: Filled with Fear and Anxiety

Daily Scripture Reading: Philippians 4:4–7

Let your gentleness be evident to all. The Lord is near. Do not be anxious about anything, but in every situation, by prayer and petition, with thanksgiving, present your requests to God. And the peace of God, which transcends all understanding, will guard your hearts and your minds in Christ Jesus. (verses 5–7)

SHE WAS SHAKING LIKE A LEAF. RHAASWARI AND TEN other national Bible translators in South Asia were receiving new computer tablets to aid in their work. She opened the box, her eyes wide as saucers. Rhaaswari was struck by the magnitude and importance of translating God's Holy Word for her people. And she was filled with fear and anxiety.

As the team of translators prayed together, seeking God's strength and the guidance of the Holy Spirit, Rhaaswari's fear and anxiety melted away. God replaced fear with peace and a dedication to translate His Holy Word. Any inadequacy she'd felt was replaced with empowerment. By the end of the workshop, Rhaaswari and her team translated the Book of Acts in their heart language.

Wycliffe Associates equips and trains national Bible translators like Rhaaswari so they can translate the Scriptures for their own people, who live in some of the most remote and persecuted places in the world. Rhaaswari and her team depend wholly on God's peace and empowerment as they continue to translate Scripture so that one day, their people will have the entire Word of God.

Today's Prayer: Dear Lord Jesus, I, too, am filled with anxiety, feeling incapable of meeting the expectations of our culture—the pressure to produce and be perfect. Oh Lord, fill me with Your peace, and empower me to do Your will. Thank you, Jesus. Amen.

Name changed for security reasons.

Day 56: Praise and Gratitude

Daily Scripture Reading: Isaiah 41:10, 13

So do not fear, for I am with you; do not be dismayed, for I am your God. I will strengthen you and help you; I will uphold you with my righteous right hand. (verse 10)

NATIONAL BIBLE TRANSLATORS AROUND THE WORLD are committed to bringing the life-giving Word of God to their people. Below, Jestle* and Arnel* share about their experience:

"Good day to you, brothers and sisters in Christ. I am from the tribe of Ik,* and I'm one of those who came to do translation recording. I continue to praise the Lord and thank Him, because I know that He is the one who helps us through the Holy Spirit during our translation of His Word. I want also to thank everyone for helping us. I believe that what we have done will help everyone who has faith in God, and that the Lord will give freedom to those who will hear what we have translated. May His name be praised forever. Hallelujah!" —Jestle

"My name is Arnel. I am a native speaker of the Cu* language, and I was one of the translators who took part in this task of translating the Bible into our language so that our own people will be able to understand more about God. Not all people are able to read and write or know how to access the Internet in order to have more knowledge about God. Bible translation is such a blessing for us, for I believe that this will widen our understanding. I thank the Lord for all of you who help us translate the Word into our language." —Arnel

Today's Prayer: Lord, like Jestle and Arnel, I know it is You who helps me and strengthens me to continue in Your will. I praise You, Lord Jesus. Amen.

*Names changed for security reasons.

Day 57: "The Word of God Is Life"

Daily Scripture Reading: Romans 12:9–21

Never be lacking in zeal, but keep your spiritual fervor, serving the Lord. Be joyful in hope, patient in affliction, faithful in prayer. (verses 11–12)

SOMETIMES NATIONAL TRANSLATION TEAMS ARRIVE for a follow-up Bible translation workshop and pick up where they left off at the previous workshop. Well, you can imagine the surprise when four teams arrived at a follow-up workshop in the Democratic Republic of the Congo with more than 70 percent of their Scripture translations already completed. What a blessing to see the enthusiasm and dedication of these translators!

Three of the groups had completely drafted the New Testament in their villages and just needed to do some additional accuracy checking and editing at the workshop. The fourth group had only three books left to translate, which they have since completed.

All four of these translation teams understand what the power of God's Word will mean for their people.

"I love this work," said one Bible translator. "I see that the Word of God is life. Praise God!"

Today's Prayer: I praise You, Lord, that Your Word is life to me, too. You give me peace and joy when I spend time with You, especially when I read the Bible. Thank you, Jesus. Amen.

Day 58: It Took a Dream

Daily Scripture Reading: John 14:5–14

Jesus answered, "I am the way and the truth and the life. No one comes to the Father except through me." (verse 6)

REVEREND KAH* HASN'T ALWAYS BEEN THE PAS-
toral type. Actually, he once was a devout Muslim who
took pleasure in persecuting the Christians in his community.
But a dream changed everything.

"One day in a dream, I saw a man come to me," Reverend
Kah recalled. "He said to me, 'I am the way, the life, and the
truth.' After that, I began to think about Christianity. My wife
and I attended a Christian church. We were attracted to the
church programs, so we kept going to the church, taking our
children with us. We did not understand well what was being
preached, so one of the church members started to teach my
family about Christ, and we started to grow in our faith.

"When the community heard that I had been converted
to Christianity, they came to my house and destroyed many
things, including my water pipe and electric power," Reverend
Kah continued. "They also stigmatized me and excluded me
from any social activities. After that, all my family left the
country. We started to live and evangelize in another Muslim
country, where thirty households have accepted Jesus Christ
as their Savior."

Recently, Reverend Kah was part of a team of national Bible translators at a translation workshop. Despite ongoing harassment from local Muslims, that team completed the New Testament in their language.

Today's Prayer: You, dear Jesus, died for me because of the love of Your Father. Jesus, You show me the truth that gives me freedom. And, Jesus, You are life everlasting. Oh, Lord Jesus, thank you! Amen.

Names changed for security reasons.

Day 59: "Bible translation brings changes to every life"

Daily Scripture Reading: Ephesians 3:14–21

Now to him who is able to do immeasurably more than all we ask or imagine, according to his power that is at work within us, to him be glory in the church and in Christ Jesus throughout all generations, for ever and ever! Amen. (verses 20–21)

A BIBLE TRANSLATION WORKSHOP FOR NINETEEN languages was held in Jelso village, Papua New Guinea, in July, 2019. Pam, along with other staff and donors, travelled there to provide prayer support.

"For two weeks we prayed for all the precious people who were there, whether they came by and asked for prayer or not," Pam recalls. "We prayer walked around Jelso village, [and] hugged on and loved all those God brought to the workshop, asking God to do great things, though not sure what He would do."

Koil, a coordinator for Bible translation in the region, reported: "Here in my community, Jelso, great things are happening—all the youth from my community started going to Sunday services, because [the] Bible translation event was important. Important believers from all over the world have put their steps on the land and turned that place into a holy place, which today I give great thanks—the Lord is good."

Koil ended his report with, "Today, youth [are] going around telling other youths that Bible translation brings changes to every life."

"Never did I think our prayers would have an impact on the youth who were not even participating in the workshop," Pam remarked. "As He always does, God did immeasurably more than all we ask or think. Amazing."

Today's Prayer: Lord, Jesus, please open my heart to pray for neighbors in my community. I know there are many who do not know You. Amen.

Day 60: Taking a Step of Faith

Daily Scripture Reading: Hebrews 13:5–6

So we say with confidence, "The Lord is my helper; I will not be afraid. What can mere mortals do to me?" (verse 6)

Ester was desperate to have God's transforming Word in her own language. She heard about an opportunity to help translate the Scriptures into her heart language. Ester felt God calling her to the work of Bible translation. She was so excited to think she could help.

Though the Bible translation workshop would be right there in the Democratic Republic of the Congo, she still had to get time off from her job as a nurse. So, Ester asked her boss for a leave of absence—and she was denied twice. Determined, Ester went to an even higher level of management in another city with her request. She again received an emphatic no.

Ester felt the presence of the Holy Spirit and knew what she would do. In a step of faith, Ester quit her job so she could translate the Bible.

Ester's passion and commitment to Bible translation caused her boss to finally grant her the leave of absence and let her know that she could keep her job. What a blessing!

Along with a team of translators, Ester helped start work on the Old Testament in their heart language. Ester was so happy to be able to bring God's Word to her people in their language.

Today's Prayer: Gracious Lord, Ester trusted You to help her give up work if she had to, so that she could respond to Your call to Bible translation. Lord, please help me do what it takes to complete the work You have given me to accomplish. In Jesus's name. Amen.

Day 61: "Pursued by God"

Daily Scripture Reading: Colossians 3:12–14

Therefore, as God's chosen people, holy and dearly loved, clothe yourselves with compassion, kindness, humility, gentleness and patience. (verse 12)

" I WAS A VERY YOUNG CHILD WHEN WE WERE FORCED to flee [a country in the Middle East]," says Haliah,* whose family made their way to the United States.

"My siblings and I were enrolled in an Islamic school here, and we were taught to recite verses from the Quran," she says. "It was a way to hold on to our faith and our culture.

"The older I got, I became more influenced by Western culture, and I began to struggle with my own identity," Haliah says. "I began to rebel against my family and Islam. Little did I know I was being pursued by God."

Today Haliah stands firm in her faith as the only Christian in her Muslim family. She prays fervently for her family and sees signs of God at work.

"They're starting to question the differences between Jesus in Islam and the Jesus in our Holy Bible," she says. "I know that one day the Lord will redeem them."

Haliah prays for her people in her home country in the Middle East—men, women, and children who don't know about the freedom that is in Christ. Christians like Haliah are grateful that Wycliffe Associates focuses on Bible translation in places closed to Christianity.

Today's Prayer: Father God, thank you for pursuing and loving me, just as You love Haliah. Please help me to share Your love with those who need You. In the name of Jesus, I pray. Amen.

Name changed for security reasons.

Day 62: A Church of Nine Languages

Daily Scripture Reading: Galatians 6:9–10

Let us not become weary in doing good, for at the proper time we will reap a harvest if we do not give up. (verse 9)

PASTOR GEORGE'S CHURCH IS COMPRISED OF PEOPLE in nine different language groups. His main mission in life is for everyone in his church to have God's Word in their heart language. He heard about Wycliffe Associates, so he set off on a half-day journey from his village in Botswana to Zambia to see what he could find out.

Along the way, Pastor George's car broke down. He missed the ferry. That meant he had to wait another day to cross the river. Then several more rides took him the rest of the way.

"I couldn't let my broken-down car stop me," says Pastor George. "I promised my church community that I would find out about Bible translation. I couldn't go home without fulfilling my promise."

A checking workshop was set to start that afternoon when Pastor George arrived. Our team explained to him the methodology, and one of the participating translators spent time walking him through the required steps for clear and accurate translation. Pastor George took what he learned and began translating Luke into Chinyanja, his heart language.

Pastor George returned home with some translated Scripture and an even greater desire for his congregation to read God's Word in their heart languages. He began training and raising up local translators. Together they translated sixteen New Testament books. Then Pastor George led Bible translation workshops for five more languages that completed the four Gospels!

Today's Prayer: Lord God, Pastor George did not give up when his travels seemed impossible. Now he's leading his people in Bible translation. Lord, help me not to give up when the Christian life feels wearisome. I pray this in Jesus's name. Amen.

Day 63: "I have never seen such hunger for God's Word."

Daily Scripture Reading: Romans 10:13–15

Everyone who calls on the name of the Lord will be saved. (verse 13)

A L, A STAFF MEMBER WITH WYCLIFFE ASSOCIATES, stood before three hundred people in a small, remote village in Madagascar. As they cheered and danced for almost fifteen minutes, Al realized that he had never seen such hunger for God's Word! All he had said to spark this celebration was that they soon would have help to get the Bible in their language of Bitsimisaraka.

But there was no Bible in Madagascar's Plateau Malagasy language, which is spoken by millions of people, that the village could use to translate the Bible into their heart language. So national translators diligently translated the Bible into Plateau Malagasy. And in the fall of 2019, they completed the Bible. That was just the beginning, because Plateau Malagasy is a gateway language and is now used as the source text to translate the Bible into Madagascar's other distinct languages.

In fact, just two weeks after the Plateau Malagasy Bible was completed, sixty national translators convened in the capital city of Antananarivo to begin Bible translation for six more language groups. Al said that "it was especially rewarding for the Plateau Malagasy translators to serve as facilitators at this

Bible translation workshop, because they could see the fruit of all their hard work."

One mother-tongue translator, who was over eighty years old, was in tears when he received his Gospel of Mark. His efforts during a workshop had produced the first Scripture he had ever seen in his heart language.

Today's Prayer: Thank you, Jesus, for the testimony of Your churches around the world who work so diligently to ensure your Word is made available to all people. Lord Jesus, give me a hunger for Your Word and a thirst that only You can quench. Amen.

Day 64: Thrilled and Encouraged

Daily Scripture Reading: James 1:16–18

Don't be deceived, my dear brothers and sisters. Every good and perfect gift is from above, coming down from the Father of the heavenly lights. (verses 16–17)

WHEN NATIONAL BIBLE TRANSLATORS IN TANZANIA arrived at the workshop, they learned how to accurately and efficiently translate God's Word into their heart languages.

But what a surprise when their eyesight was tested! Many national translators live in poverty in rural villages, and women especially have many eyesight problems.

Of the forty-seven translators tested at this workshop, twenty-seven showed a dire need for reading glasses. So, those translators were fitted and given new eyeglasses.

What a great gift and blessing to these dedicated national Bible translators! They were thrilled with their new glasses and so encouraged to be better equipped to work toward their goal of God's Word in their languages. Several of these same language groups have a completed translation of the New Testament, and they are now translating the Old Testament for their people.

Today's Prayer: We praise You, Lord God, for blessing these wonderfully dedicated translators who are bringing Your

Word to their people. I thank you today, dear Lord, for Your gifts and blessings in my life. You are so good and such a wonderful Father. In the name of Jesus, I pray. Amen.

Day 65: "We really need this"

Daily Bible Reading: 2 Timothy 3:14–17

All Scripture is God-breathed and is useful for teaching, rebuking, correcting and training in righteousness, so that the servant of God may be thoroughly equipped for every good work. (verses 16–17)

TODAY WYCLIFFE ASSOCIATES EMPOWERS AND equips national Bible translators—native speakers—to translate the Scriptures into their heart language through workshops under the guidance and authority of the local church.

Following a Bible translation workshop in the Philippines, messages of gratitude for you were received from people who were grateful for their newly translated Scripture. Here are their words:

"I am Alfredo Bumaynin, and I want to express my sincere gratitude to this organization of Bible translation. Translating the Bible into our language is a great opportunity for us. We will be able to know and understand more about the Scriptures. And I believe that more and more souls in our tribe will be saved because of this Bible translation in our language."

"For the past seventeen years, I, Pastor Jose Ananayo, have been preaching the Good News to my people. I know they could not fully understand the Scriptures, because we've been using a Bible that is different from our language. This Bible translation into our language is a necessity for us. We really need this, because people will be able to understand more about the Word of God—not only in our church, but for all people who can understand our language. Bless you!"

Today's Prayer: Thank you, Jesus, that Your Word teaches me how to live and prepares me for the work You want me to do. I pray You will bless the work of my hands. In Your name, Jesus. Amen.

Day 66: "We're all ordinary Christians."

Daily Scripture Reading: 1 Corinthians 2:1–5

I came to you in weakness with great fear and trembling. My message and my preaching were not with wise and persuasive words, but with a demonstration of the Spirit's power, so that your faith might not rest on human wisdom, but on God's power. (verses 3–5)

"HOW COULD IT BE TRUE?" PASTOR ISRAELI wondered.

"I never believed my team could do this work, because we're all ordinary Christians," Pastor Israeli says. "This is a miracle to me."

Indeed, God works through "ordinary" Christians on a regular basis, but His work is nothing short of extraordinary. In fact, Pastor Israeli's team was one of three Tanzanian teams from a recent Bible translation event to complete their New Testament.

Imagine finally being able to read and hear God's precious Word for the first time. Without question, the greatest tool for evangelism—the Bible in the heart language—is easier to understand and is the guiding truth for living a godly life.

Today's Prayer: Heavenly Father, just as Pastor Israeli remarked, we are ordinary Christians whom You empower to do Your work. I pray, Lord, that I will continue to depend on the power of God through the Holy Spirit as I work. In Jesus's Name. Amen.

Day 67: It Has Made All the Difference

Daily Scripture Reading: Nehemiah 4:16–23

Wherever you hear the sound of the trumpet, join us there. Our God will fight for us. So we continued the work. (verses 20-21)

EVERY DAY FOLLOWING A LONG DAY OF TRANSLATION work during a Malaysia Bible translation workshop, Robert wrote in his journal. Here is an entry he wrote about the prayer warriors:

"We have two full-time prayer warriors that have accompanied us from halfway around the world. It has made all the difference. On August 1 while preparing for this Bible translation trip, one of our warriors wanted to ready herself for spiritual battle. She prayed specifically over Nehemiah's verses at the rebuilding of the wall when faced with great opposition:

Then I said to the nobles, the officials and the rest of the people, 'The work is extensive and spread out, and we are widely separated from each other along the wall. Wherever you hear the sound of the trumpet, join us there. Our God will fight for us!'

So we continued the work with half the men holding spears, from the first light of dawn till the stars came out. (verses 19–21)

"Today at 6:43 p.m. she shared this testimony and a reading of the English version just as I was scanning the new translation of that *same* chapter for storage into the cloud for safekeeping. Just *two* minutes later, our Asian translator came forward and publicly read this passage for the *first* time in their language. We serve an awesome God!"

Today's Prayer: Lord, there are times when I am doing Your work, yet I feel oppressed by the Evil One. I pray, Lord God, that You will protect me and fight for me. In those moments, remind me of the truth through Your Word.

Day 68: "When they hear it, they will believe in the Lord."

Daily Scripture Reading: Romans 10:8–15

If you declare with your mouth, "Jesus is Lord," and believe in your heart that God raised him from the dead, you will be saved. (verse 9)

HOPE* LIVES IN THE PHILIPPINES. SHE IS PASSIONATE about sharing God's Word with her people, so she attended a Wycliffe Associates Church Owned Bible Translation workshop and became a Bible translator. The following is an excerpt from the note Hope sent to Wycliffe Associates:

"I have learned a lot of things during the workshop. I can say that, because I did not expect that a Bible translation in our own language K* will happen.

"When we go home to our place, I would be happy to share about the things we did and learned in this workshop. I will also teach what I have learned here to the kids. I will share this in our church and request that we should have a Bible study for the children so we can teach them using our K New Testament. We are so thankful for this opportunity to translate the New Testament in our own language.

"There are a lot of people who read the Bible, but they cannot understand, because it is not of their own language. So, we are very thankful that the K New Testament has been made available. When we're done translating it, I will share it in our village and let them hear it. And I pray and believe that when they hear it, they will believe in the Lord."

Today's Prayer: Lord, thank you for Bible translators who work to share Your Word, for You desire that all should be saved. Show me today with whom I can share Your Word. Lord, make my words be filled with Your love today. I ask this in Jesus's name. Amen.

Names changed for security reasons.

Day 69: Once Skeptical, Now a Strong Believer

Daily Scripture Reading: Mark 10:17–27

Jesus looked at them and said, "With man this is impossible, but not with God; all things are possible with God." (verse 27)

Pastor Milton longed for the Bible to be translated into his heart language. His deepest desire was to see his congregation reading and understanding God's Word for themselves. Pastor Milton prayed for years, even though he had been told that Bible translation would be too costly and would take many years to translate just one book of the Bible. It seemed impossible, yet he persevered in prayer.

Wycliffe Associates introduced Church Owned Bible Translation to the Ugandan churches in 2018. Pastor Milton attended that first workshop, though he was skeptical that the eight steps of the translation methodology actually would help the people get the Bible into their heart language. And following the instructions of his facilitator at the workshop, he actually translated both 1 and 2 Peter.

Later, in the spring of 2021, the New Testament was printed for community checking before publication. The result of the first community check was revival. God answered the longing of Pastor Milton's heart—Scripture in his heart language!

Now a strong believer in Church Owned Bible Translation methods, Pastor Milton goes to neighboring language groups, teaching the church leaders and pastors how to translate the Bible for their people. Today he is a strong believer that every home should have the Bible in their heart language. And this is the very vision of Wycliffe Associates: a Bible in every language.

Today's Prayer: Faithful God, I pray for national Bible translators. So many face seemingly impossible odds. Keep us faithful to our part in the task of advancing Bible translation so that all may have Your Word in their heart language. In Jesus's name I pray. Amen.

Day 70: Making the Most of an Opportunity

Daily Scripture Reading: Ephesians 5:15–21

Be very careful, then, how you live—not as unwise but as wise, making the most of every opportunity, because the days are evil. Therefore do not be foolish, but understand what the Lord's will is. (verses 15–17)

IN MARCH, 2020, ALL AROUND THE WORLD, COUN-tries were locking down their borders due to the COVID-19 pandemic. During that same month, Wycliffe Associates was holding Church Owned Bible Translation workshops in six countries in Southern Africa for seventeen language groups. The workshop in Namibia ended two days early so that the Bible translators could return to their home countries.

However, the Namibian border officially closed before two Wycliffe Associates team members were able to cross to return home. They were stuck. They discovered a nearby campground, complete with cabins, and they began to think about how they might use this time.

They realized that three of the Bible translation teams whom they had just trained lived nearby. So, they invited five translators from each language group to join them at the campground for an additional workshop.

Excitement grew as they all realized the opportunity God brought to them. Each translator worked on a portion of Scripture in his own room, and then each team would gather outdoors following the social distancing guidelines to do their verse-by-verse checking.

By the time the borders reopened and our two team members could return to their countries, the three teams had made great strides in their Bible translations. The two translation teams each completed eight New Testament books. The third group finished six books!

Today's Prayer: Dear Jesus, help me use my time wisely and live out my day accomplishing the work You have for me to do. Make me a blessing to those in my life. Show me how I can help advance Bible translation so that all can have Your Word in their heart language. Thank you, Jesus. Amen.

Day 71: She Listened . . . and Felt Joy!

Daily Scripture Reading: 1 Peter 1:3–9

Though you have not seen him, you love him; and even though you do not see him now, you believe in him and are filled with an inexpressible and glorious joy. (verse 8)

SONYA* LIVED MOST OF HER LIFE IN A SMALL VILLAGE in Africa. She was uneducated and didn't know much about Jesus. But that changed when she heard audio recordings of the New Testament in her heart language. Consumed by the Good News she was hearing, Sonya listened to the Scripture recordings again and again. She couldn't get enough.

Sonya watched a missionary friend stop and pray for people in her village. She asked this friend if only certain people could follow Jesus. She was thrilled to learn that Jesus is for everyone. Sonya was amazed, saying, "Jesus is wonderful. Jesus is great. This is such good news."

She not only decided to follow Christ, but she wanted others to know about Him too. She invited local women and children into her modest home to listen to the Scripture recordings. When everyone in her village had heard the gospel, she started visiting nearby villages that had not yet heard about Jesus. Sonya shared with them what she had learned from the Word of God in her heart language.

Followers of Christ like Sonya are deeply grateful for God's translated Word and the good news of Jesus's love and sacrifice that is for everyone.

Today's Prayer: Father God, I do believe that Your sacrifice of Jesus was so that we can be your children. Father, please fill me with joy like Sonya's when I am reading and sharing Your Word. Thank you, Father. Amen.

Name changed for security reasons.

Day 72: "We can take responsibility"

Daily Scripture Reading: Matthew 28:16–20

All authority in heaven and on earth has been given to me. Therefore go and make disciples of all nations, baptizing them in the name of the Father and of the Son and of the Holy Spirit, and teaching them to obey everything I have commanded you. (verses 18–20)

AROUND THE WORLD, WORD IS SPREADING THAT Church Owned Bible Translation is the way for all people groups to have the Word of God in their heart language. Wycliffe Associates empowers and equips native speakers through Bible translation workshops. They are using resources and tools created by linguists and software specialists so they can accurately translate all of Scripture into their heart languages.

"Church Owned Bible Translation is giving the church authority to know they are part of this vision," says Pastor Buster from Livingstone, Zambia. "It's a way of helping people understand that we can do it in partnership with the visionaries of this work, and we can take responsibility."

In Zambia, pastors and church leaders from many denominations have been using the translation and discipleship training to see their Bible translation project as their very own. Pastor Buster and his team have taken the responsibility to translate the Bible into their language and then helped five other language groups in Zambia complete the Bible in their languages. Now, four more people groups in Southern Africa are at work, getting the Bible into their heart languages.

Today's Prayer: Thank you, Jesus, for Pastor Buster's example as he lives out Your command to "make disciples of all nations." I pray for him as he continues to faithfully assist language groups in Zambia and other countries to translate the Scriptures into all the languages of Southern Africa. Lord Jesus, help me to be an encourager to Bible translators around the world by actively praying for them and their work.

Day 73: "Don't you dare stop!"

Daily Scripture Reading: Ephesians 3:14–21

I pray that you, being rooted and established in love, may have power, together with all the Lord's holy people, to grasp how wide and long and high and deep is the love of Christ, and to know this love that surpasses knowledge—that you may be filled to the measure of all the fullness of God. (verses 17–19)

CALA'S HUSBAND BAASHIR* IS A BIBLE TRANSLATOR for the Pi* language group in Central Asia. Cala* just didn't see the point of another version of the Scriptures. "Could it really be that different?" she wondered. "We have the Urdu Bible," Cala said with a hint of scorn. "We have the English Bible. We do not need another translation!"

Then one day she walked into the couple's living room and asked Baashir what he was reading. He explained that for his morning devotions, he was reading fifteen chapters of a typed copy from the Pi New Testament that he was helping to translate.

Curiosity got the best of Cala, and she began reading over her husband's shoulder. In an instant, everything she had thought and said about another translation no longer applied. Suddenly God's Word seemed incredibly new, and it pierced Cala's heart.

Cala grabbed the pages of Scripture from Baashir's hands and held them close. "I have read that passage so many times before," she said, "but it's so much easier to understand in my own language. You *must* do this work! Don't you dare stop!"

Baashir hasn't stopped. The fifty-eight million Pi speakers soon will be better able to experience the fullness of God because His Word is in their heart language.

Today's Prayer: Come Holy Spirit, and be my guide as I read God's Word. Please fill me with the love of Jesus Christ so that I may know and love You more. In Jesus's name. Amen.

Names changed for security reasons.

Day 74: "Something was different."

Daily Scripture Reading: Ephesians 4:1–6

As a prisoner for the Lord, then, I urge you to live a life worthy of the calling you have received. (verse 1)

GROWING UP IN AN ISLAMIC COUNTRY, AYAAN* determined that religion was pointless, even his own. As far as Ayaan was concerned, religion was not the answer to the world's problems. Religion was *the* problem.

A close friend quietly let Ayaan know that he had accepted Jesus. Ayaan couldn't believe his ears. What a stupid thing to do, he thought. Strong in his newfound faith, the friend handed Ayaan a New Testament and suggested that he read it. It changed everything in Ayaan's life.

"The next morning, at 6:00 a.m., it was like some strange power woke me up," Ayaan says. "I woke up reading my new book. When I read Jesus's Sermon on the Mount, that really penetrated my heart. All the ideas I had about religion changed. The next morning, it was the same—up and reading at 6:00 a.m., which is so strange for me, because I never wake up early."

This continued for ten days. Ayaan devoured the New Testament and prayed a prayer of repentance. "It was a turning point for me," he says. "Something was different. Lots of joy came into my life, and I knew I really needed whatever Jesus had offered me."

Soon after his acceptance of Christ, Ayaan was jailed, beaten, and tortured for his new faith in Jesus. Still strong in faith, he eventually was released from jail and escaped to another country.

Once freed from his persecutors, Ayaan began a ministry to train refugees from his homeland. These trained refugees then will return home and spread the gospel. Ayaan says of his mission, "I have a passion to share God's Word with everybody in my home country."

Today's Prayer: Lord Jesus, may all persecuted believers soon have Your encouraging Words of love and grace. Amen.

Name changed for security reasons.

Day 75—"We are being united."

Daily Scripture Reading: John 15:5–12

If you keep my commands, you will remain in my love, just as I have kept my Father's commands and remain in his love. I have told you this so that my joy may be in you and that your joy may be complete. (verses 10–11)

THE 120,000 Sa* MEN, WOMEN, AND CHILDREN living in Asia have the Scriptures only in the regional trade language, not in their language.

The Sa national Bible translation team recently received new laptop computers and Bible translation training during a Wycliffe Associates workshop. This equipment, loaded with Bible translation resources, has helped them do the hard work of translation accurately and efficiently. By God's grace and mercy, the New Testament now is being translated into the language they know and love.

God is blessing the Sa translators near and far as they experience great unity in their shared goal.

"It has been a blessed moment since we started translating the Word of God into our heart language," says one translator. "Despite the pandemic, we are continuously having Sa fellowship, virtually, every Sunday evening. Sa believers from different parts inside our country and even abroad are participating. We are being united because our people are interested in the translated Scriptures, and we can now pray in our language and preach as well. We are thankful to God for making this possible through Wycliffe Associates."

All who are united together in Jesus Christ experience great joy when God's Holy Word is being shared together in the heart language of the people.

Today's Prayer: Dear Lord, there is joy in my heart knowing that believers are sharing newly translated Scripture in their heart language during virtual online calls with one another. In praise to You, Lord Jesus. Amen.

Names changed for security reasons.

Day 76: "I know . . . that God wants to use me."

Daily Scripture Reading: 2 Peter 3:11–18

But grow in the grace and knowledge of our Lord and Savior Jesus Christ. To him be glory both now and forever! Amen. (verse 18)

FIJI IS A BEAUTIFUL ISLAND NATION IN THE PACIFIC, with white sandy beaches that meet crystal blue waters. Countless vacationers call it paradise on earth.

But living in this beautiful land are people still without God's Word in their heart language—people still waiting to read the good news of Jesus's love and mercy. On the islands, God has raised up a new generation of national Bible translators who are deeply committed to bringing His Word to their people.

"When our youth leader announced a Bible translation workshop during the school holiday, I was excited and asked my father if I could attend," says Sandra. She is the daughter of a local pastor and one of many young people who gave up their school break to be trained in Bible translation methods. With expert guidance and instruction, the young translators helped complete wonderful first drafts of Galatians, Romans, and 1 Corinthians. Out of their Bible translation experience grew a deep passion to reach their families, friends, and community with God's Word in their heart language.

"I know that I have a calling on my life and that God wants to use me," Sandra says. "I wish to be part of the Bible translation team and to teach other language groups who wish to translate the Bible in their own heart language."

Passionate young Bible translators like Sandra are certain to help their neighbors and friends translate God's Word for their people.

Today's Prayer: Oh God, I pray for the young people around the world, that soon they all will have Your Word in their heart languages. I pray for those like Sandra who are investing their lives in Your work and purpose. May they grow in grace and in the knowledge of You, Lord Jesus. Amen.

Day 77: "Will you please help us?"

Daily Scripture Reading: Hebrews 13:1–3

Continue to remember those in prison as if you were together with them in prison, and those who are mistreated as if you yourselves were suffering. (verse 3)

THE SECRET MESSAGE CAME FROM THREE PASTORS requesting a covert meeting—but not inside a restaurant or building where they might be identified. They only would meet us outside in an airport parking lot where they would not be recognized, and the overflying jets would keep anyone from hearing their conversation.

The actual location cannot be mentioned, but we can tell you it was an African country where Wycliffe Associates safely conducts Bible translation workshops. The three pastors are from a neighboring country where Christianity is not allowed! That's why they had to slip through an unguarded section of the border. These three courageous pastors accepted the risk, the threat of imprisonment, torture, and even death, desperately pleading, "Will you please help us translate God's Word into the heart language of our people?"

National Bible translators from these pastors' home country have been trained in Bible translation and are making wonderful progress. During the training workshop, they drafted the Book of Philemon and made plans to start Bible translation projects for twelve language groups in the region. These committed Bible translators will need our constant prayers as they move forward.

At another workshop in the area, several participating national Bible translators shared how they have been arrested and jailed for their faith. For Christians in their part of the world, it's really not a question of *if* they will go to jail, but *when*.

Today's Prayer: Oh, Holy Father, Your good news is for everyone. Jesus died and rose again so that each of us can know You. Please make a way, Father, for people in countries of persecution sharing Your good news with their families and friends. Amen.

Day 78: A Silver Lining to the Pandemic?

Daily Scripture Reading: Psalm 13

But I trust in your unfailing love; my heart rejoices in your salvation. I will sing the LORD's praise, for he has been good to me. (verses 5–6)

A DEAF OWNED BIBLE TRANSLATION TRAINING workshop was held in early 2020 for seven sign languages in Africa. Committed teams of sign language translators gathered to begin working on their New Testaments, and they made great progress. When businesses and schools began shutting down due to COVID-19, many translators used the extra time to accelerate their translation efforts. And, through the Wycliffe Associates Emergency 911 Fund, made possible by friends like you, they each received much-needed bags of food to help their families.

A Church Owned Bible Translation workshop for the Siswati language group of Eswatini (formerly Swaziland), was cut short due to COVID-19 restrictions. The diligent group of national translators already had completed 42 percent of their New Testament, and they were eager to keep the momentum going despite the limited travel and gatherings. The Wycliffe Associates team in Eswatini asked themselves why they should let the laptops that were used during training collect dust. So, working on the laptops, the Bible translators continued translating God's Word from their homes.

The Wycliffe Associates team heard that the translators were in dire need of assistance, so they encouraged the translators to upload their work to the online Bible database, which was developed to securely preserve translators' work.

We recently received word that the Eswatini Bible translators completed their New Testament and are now translating the Old Testament into their heart language.

What a silver lining to the pandemic that God's Word continued to be translated into heart languages!

Today's Prayer: Ever-giving God, thank you that even in a pandemic, Your love shined through the strife. Please bless these Deaf translators who are willing to keep at the hard work of Bible translation into their sign language. Amen.

Day 79: "We have a vision to share the Word of God"

Daily Scripture Reading: 1 John 3:1-3

See what great love the Father has lavished on us, that we should be called children of God! And that is what we are! The reason the world does not know us is that it did not know him. (verse 1)

THEY TREATED THE FI* TRIBE WITH CONTEMPT! 200,000 nomads who were made to feel "less than," could be beaten or even worse any time—even for having Scriptures of a majority language in their hands.

"My wife and I were Muslim," Pastor T* says. "But God accepted us as His children, and we're so happy after receiving new life. Now we have a vision to share the Word of God with the Fi people."

Pastor T was asked by Wycliffe Associates to help train the Fi Bible translation team who wanted a Bible in their own language. Pastor T was so excited to be asked to do the very thing he was sure God wanted him to do!

"I was filled with thanksgiving to the Lord during translation and accuracy checking," Pastor T says. "I knew in my heart the Fi people will get much blessing, and that their lives will be changed according to the Word of God."

The Fi Bible translation team have completed the New Testament in their own language. They continue to work, translating the Old Testament while at the same time producing audio recording of all the books of the Bible that they have translated.

Today's Prayer: Dear Heavenly Father, thank You for Your great love for us. Thank You for accepting us as Your children. Please help me to do what is right by loving those thought to be "less than" in my community. In Jesus's name. Amen.

Names changed for security reasons.

Day 80: Encouraged to Serve Him More

Daily Scripture Reading: 1 Thessalonians 5:4–13

Therefore encourage one another and build each other up, just as in fact you are doing. (verse 11)

AFTER MUCH INTENSIVE TRAINING AND HARD WORK, twenty-five mother tongue Bible translators in the Philippines completed their oral translation of the New Testament in their heart language of Cortesanon.

The following are notes of gratitude from two translators for Wycliffe Associates' team of leaders and facilitators:

"I am Mailyn. I am married and have five children. This workshop encouraged me to continue my life and serve the Lord more. Through His Word, I became even more motivated to do this task. I am looking forward to see[ing] my own tribe hear our recorded Bible and be saved. I am grateful that this organization has a heart to reach people groups like ours and help us have our own Bible. I am also thankful for all the facilitators who supported us [during] the entire workshop. May the Lord continue to bless you. Thank you!" –Mailyn

"I am very grateful for the Bible translation of the Cortesanon language. I was able to reflect on every word that I translated. And through the Bible stories told by the facilitators, I feel refreshed and encouraged to trust God more, even during the trials. The training event taught me new things that lighten up my mind and heart. I am blessed that I met an organization that is willing to reach out to a people group like ours and grateful our pastor approached me to be part of this work. Thank you, and God bless!" –Sheila

Today's Prayer: Dear Father, thank you for Mailyn and Sheila's blessed experience in translating Your Word. I pray that Your Word will be an encouragement to each one in my church family and that together, we will grow in our desire to serve You more. In Jesus's name. Amen

Day 81: By the Grace of God, Everyone Escaped

Daily Scripture Reading: Psalm 43

Why, my soul, are you downcast? Why so disturbed within me? Put your hope in God, for I will yet praise him, my Savior and my God. (verse 5)

BENITA IS A NATIONAL BIBLE TRANSLATOR FOR A language group in the Democratic Republic of the Congo. The sixty-year-old woman has a huge heart, loving the thirteen orphaned children in her care. You can imagine her terror when she was awakened one night by raging flames and billowing smoke. How would she get all the kids out safely?

By the grace of God, everyone escaped without injury. But the fire and smoke destroyed everything. Clothes, shoes, beds, school bags, cookware, and school uniforms all went up in flames. A local pastor and Bible translator took the entire family into his home when he realized they had nowhere to go.

The pastor fed the children and bought them shoes. Then he reached out to Wycliffe Associates to see if we could help.

Through our Emergency 911 Fund—established through the generosity of caring partners like you—Wycliffe Associates provided this hurting family with clothes, school uniforms, mattresses, blankets, hygiene supplies, and all the children's school fees.

For the first time since the fire, Benita smiled when she learned of these gifts to her family. She was deeply touched that people would give from their hearts to help her and the children. "May God be glorified," she said. "May Wycliffe Associates be blessed. Thank you for all your prayers to God on my behalf."

Please pray that the Bible translation project that is near and dear to Benita's heart will continue strong until all Scripture is in their heart language.

Today's Prayer: Though stressed and burdened, I choose to put my hope in You, my Lord and Savior. I praise You, Lord Jesus, for Your presence in my life. Thank you for the faithfulness of Benita, her church, and their team as they translate Your Word. Amen.

Day 82: Healing Bridges

Daily Scripture Reading: Psalm 31:13–24

But I trust in you, Lord; I say, "You are my God. My times are in your hands; deliver me from the hands of my enemies, from those who pursue me. Let your face shine on your servant; save me in your unfailing love." (verses 14–16)

A CHURCH OWNED BIBLE TRANSLATION WORKSHOP went to the very small community of believers in Asia, determined to get God's Word in their language. Just a handful of believers arrived to take part in the workshop. But they had also invited a few Buddhist friends along who had a strong grasp of the language and a willingness to help. As they worked through the Scriptures, God spoke to them in a personal way. After only a few days of translating His Word, four of the Buddhist participants accepted Jesus into their hearts and were baptized.

Word soon got out to the Buddhists in the community who then led a wave of persecution against the Christians for more than nine months. Then COVID-19 struck.

The effects of the pandemic hit the entire language group very hard, leaving families struggling to afford food. Many of these were the very people who were persecuting the Christians. By God's grace, partners like you raised special Emergency 911 funds and blessed 150 families in their time of need.

You showed compassion to the believers and Bible translators, and they showed kindness to those neighbors who were persecuting them. Healing bridges have been built in the community, and the persecution of Christians has ceased. More people in their community want to know the God who was responsible for this generous outpouring of kindness.

Today's Prayer: You are my God. You save me from those who would do harm with Your unfailing love. I pray that Your love will overflow to those around me today, as it did for these persecuted Bible translators in Asia. Amen.

Day 83: "We have no greater joy than this!"

Daily Scripture Reading: Isaiah 55:8–12

So is my word that goes out from my mouth: It will not return to me empty, but will accomplish what I desire and achieve the purpose for which I sent it. You will go out in joy and be led forth in peace. (verses 11–12)

THE V* PEOPLE IN INDIA THOUGHT THEY NEVER would have a Bible in their heart language. Impoverished and persecuted, the V often were ridiculed and cast aside as "gypsies." But full of enthusiasm, they participated in a Church Owned Bible Translation workshop.

During the event, the Gospel of Mark was successfully translated and recorded to audio files for all to hear. Even when COVID-19 hit, the team of Bible translators continued on their own, gradually working through the books of the New Testament.

Now the V New Testament has been completed, and it couldn't have happened to a more grateful people. Below are some of their expressions of gratitude:

"Only now are we able to understand the deeper meanings in the Word of God. Since the Bible is in our language, we are able to understand it better and grow in our spiritual life as well. I don't have words to express my joy." —Shalini

"People outside of our community have never cared or helped us. Wycliffe Associates has taken immense efforts to help us translate the Bible in our own language, have shown us the methods, and taught us as well. Now we can tell the gospel message to our people in our own language. God's Word will never perish." —Kumar

"Our children will also be able to read and learn the Word of God more than what we know. We have no greater joy than this!" —Khusboo

Today's Prayer: Oh Lord Jesus, there is no greater joy than when children hear Your Word and believe. I pray that through Bible translation, Your Word will indeed bring joy to the hearts of all who hear Your Word in their mother tongue and believe. In Jesus's name I pray. Amen.

Name changed for security reasons.

Day 84: The Gospel of Jesus Christ, Printed!

Daily Scripture Reading: John 3:16–21

For God so loved the world that he gave his one and only Son, that whoever believes in him shall not perish but have eternal life. (verse 16)

Bita* has lived a hard life. As a young child growing up in an oppressive country in the Middle East, she watched in horror as a religious leader killed her innocent father and left her family in broken shambles. In the years that followed, she came to understand that being a woman in this part of the world is extremely difficult.

After Bita married, she and her husband fled their homeland to escape persecution and seek a better, safer life. It was during their time as refugees that they were invited to a church and came to trust Jesus as their Savior. "When I prayed, I felt peace, and my life changed because I now know the one true God," Bita said.

As a new believer, Bita was filled with joy and hope that can only be found in Jesus. Even so, her heart was heavy, because God's Word had not been translated into her heart language. Yearning to have the Scriptures in the language she understands best, Bita connected with a group of translators. The Gospel of John was translated in her mother tongue and printed using the Print On Demand equipment so she could share the Gospel.

"Bible translation will make my heart stronger," Bita says. "And it is important to me so that my mother, brother, and family can read God's Word and believe in Jesus."

Today's Prayer: Lord, I pray for believers like Bita in the Middle East who are sharing the Gospel of Jesus Christ. I pray many will choose to believe in You, the one true God. In Jesus's Name. Amen

Names changed for security reasons.

Day 85: "Start reading the Bible."

Daily Scripture Reading: Romans 1:14–17

For I am not ashamed of the gospel, because it is the power of God that brings salvation to everyone who believes. (verse 16)

Pastor T,* a national Bible translator for the Fi' language, and his family lived with death threats and actual attempts on their lives. Recently, the family's water supply was poisoned, and they had to be hospitalized for immediate treatment. But Pastor T was not shaken. He has witnessed firsthand the life-changing power of the Scriptures in his heart language.

Pastor T grew up in a strict Muslim household. He had a Christian schoolteacher in eighth grade. "[My teacher] started to pray and fast for me," Pastor T said, "and I began to see dreams . . . Jesus standing with me while I'm preaching among my tribal people. I told my teacher this would never happen, as I swore to be a committed Muslim. But he never gave up on me, and he encouraged me to start reading the Bible."

After reading the Scriptures in the national language, Pastor T finally gave his life to Jesus. He remembers, "I got very excited about preaching. There was only one thing on my mind: help every single person I encounter to become a Christian."

Pastor T went on to Bible school and now pastors a church. He's also an integral part of a team that is translating

God's Word for his people. With training from Wycliffe Associates, Pastor T has helped translate the New Testament into the Fi language. And his team is committed to continue until they have a complete Bible!

Today's Prayer: Faithful God, through translation of Your Word into the heart languages, people can understand Your Word, believe, and be saved. I pray today that Bible translators around the world will have success in bringing the entire Word of God to their people, in their language. Amen.

Names changed for security reasons.

Day 86: Sometimes It Takes Courage and Determination

Daily Scripture Reading: Hebrews 6:9–12

God is not unjust; he will not forget your work and the love you have shown him as you have helped his people and continue to help them. (verse 10)

FOR SECURITY PURPOSES WE CANNOT NAME THE Re* translators or the language group. They are committed believers determined to have the Bible in their heart language.

The Re believers were invited to attend a Wycliffe Associates Bible translation workshop. In order to attend, they would first take a journey that pushed their limits. It would be physically exhausting and downright dangerous at times. Yet, with total determination and the Lord's protection, the Re national translators set out to accomplish the task God had prepared for them.

For seven long days, these Christians traveled by foot, each weighed down carrying their own food, water, and other vital supplies. They walked all day and slept at night in dark jungles under the stars, wary of tigers known to prowl the region. They prayed for God's protection.

The week-long walk then was followed by an overnight bus ride. When the group arrived at the Bible translation workshop, they knew in their hearts the result would be well worth their difficult journey. They were right. During the workshop they were trained to do Bible translation and record their work using BTRKs (Bible Translation Recording Kits). Once home, they dedicated their time to Bible translation and completed the recording of their audio New Testament.

Sometimes it takes courageous national Bible translators like these to bring God's Word of hope to their people.

Today's Prayer: Almighty God, thank you for giving the Re believers strength and stamina to bring Your words of love to their people. Lord, please give me strength to endure the difficulties in my life with grace. Please use me to help others with greater needs, and empower me to help with love and a gracious spirit. In Jesus's name. Amen.

Name changed for security reasons.

Day 87: "Knowing this has brought us much joy."

Daily Scripture Reading: Colossians 2:1–7

My goal is that they may be encouraged in heart and united in love, so that they may have the full riches of complete understanding, in order that they may know the mystery of God, namely, Christ, in whom are hidden all the treasures of wisdom and knowledge. (verses 2–3)

JAHAN,* A BIBLE TRANSLATOR, ATTENDED A BIBLE translation workshop. In the following message, he shares his gratitude after his team completed the New Testament in their language:

"We have been working hard to share the gospel of Jesus Christ with the Za* people. The materials you have given us to translate have brought much joy to many people. They have been motivated to listen and study the Word of God. Even some of the people who have been believers for a long time contacted us to let us know that for the first time, they have been able to study the books of Romans and Exodus in their entirety. It was too difficult for them to study these books in the trade language. But by listening in Za, they have found it easier to understand. Knowing this has brought us much joy.

"Interestingly, once they have read about Jesus in their own language, Za people who have never shown any interest in Christianity often ask for more literature or audio tapes, which we are happy to give to them.

"This has been a blessing for many Za people. Thank you for all you have done. Thank you to all the people who have made this possible. The grace and the peace of our Lord be with you."

Today's Prayer: Help me, Lord, to study Scripture and understand what You want me to know. Thank You for the Za Bible translators who have brought Your Word to their people so they, too, can experience the joy that can only come from God's Word. I pray in Jesus's name. Amen.

Names changed for security reasons.

Day 88: His Word Is More Precious than Gold

Daily Scripture Reading: Psalm 19:7–14

The decrees of the LORD are firm, and all of them are righteous. They are more precious than gold, than much pure gold; they are sweeter than honey, than honey from the honeycomb. (verses 9–10)

THEIR CRY WAS DESPERATE: "WE NEED BIBLES. WE need the whole Bible." Several families of new believers formed an underground house church in a volatile country in the Middle East. The logistics of getting Bibles to these families would be extremely dangerous. We knew we had to try.

The Scriptures this young church was using were what they had managed to print from the Internet. They had printed only one copy for the families to divide up and secretly pass around. They would take turns reading and studying. They yearned for the whole truth of God's Word and wanted just ten Bibles—one for each family.

We began reaching out to contacts. Plans were put into place through a series of covert messages and coded communications, and before too long, the Bibles were sent off on a five-week journey.

Once the Bibles made it inside the country, they had to be hand carried five hundred miles to the drop-off site. This was the most dangerous part of the operation, as being caught with even one Bible could result in imprisonment or worse.

But God in His faithfulness protected each person carrying the Bibles through the entire journey.

When the Bibles arrived at this isolated little church, the joy of the new believers who received them was palpable. This was the first time they had ever seen a complete Bible, the first time they had ever held one in their hands. And now each household has a copy of God's Word to keep secret, to read, and to study with their families.

Today's Prayer: Dear Father God, the Bible tells of the sacrifice of Your Son because of Your great love. Oh Father, Your Words in my language are precious and so sweet. And now this little church has the opportunity to read and study Your precious Word. Amen.

Day 89: "Choose God's light and then share it."

Daily Scripture Reading: 1 Thessalonians 1:2–10

You became imitators of us and of the Lord, for you welcomed the message in the midst of severe suffering with the joy given by the Holy Spirit. (verse 6)

DALIL* IS A DEDICATED MEMBER OF A WYCLIFFE Associates Bible translation team in a Middle Eastern country. Here, in this interview, he shares the importance of the Bible in his heart language.

Wycliffe Associates: "What is the situation regarding Bible translation in your part of the world?"

Dalil: "My home country is large, with about eighty million people, and they are under the rule of Islam. They have no idea about Christianity or who Jesus is. With training from Wycliffe Associates, I'm able to translate books of the Bible from English into my mother tongue."

Wycliffe Associates: "Why are you willing to risk your life for the gospel?"

Dalil: "I know it's risky, but I have to do this. In Matthew 28:19, God says to us, 'Go and make disciples of all nations.'

If we don't, all the people in my homeland are going to die without Jesus. I have to tell them about the real God."

Wycliffe Associates: "What is your goal as you proceed with Bible translation?"

Dalil: "In my home city, the young people don't have any hope for the future. The community is so sad, so dark. They don't know what joy is. My goal is for a young person from each family to choose God's light and then share it with their family so they can all have hope in Jesus."

Today's Prayer: Dear Heavenly Father, please help Dalil continue to shine the light of Your gospel in his home country and community. Especially, Lord, bring hope to the youth. Please help me to listen to Your message, to be filled with joy, and share the hope I have in Jesus. In Jesus's name. Amen.

Name changed for security reasons.

Day 90: "My role in Bible translation . . ."

Daily Scripture Reading: 1 Peter 4:7–19

Each of you should use whatever gift you have received to serve others, as faithful stewards of God's grace in its various forms. (verse 10)

TOMUSSONE NEARLY DIED OF A DRUG OVERDOSE. But then he decided to become a follower of Jesus Christ. "I was in the hospital for more than two weeks," he says, "and when I was discharged, I realized that God had given me another chance. I started to believe that He had something for me to do."

God was not finished with Tomussone. In 2016, this man from Mozambique attended a Bible translation workshop. He had never used a computer before, but as he listened in on a technology training session during the workshop, the Holy Spirit seemed to tell him, "You can do this!"

Following the training session, the facilitator gave Tomussone a thumb drive loaded with additional training materials about information technology. Borrowing a friend's computer, he spent his free time studying and learning.

Today, Tomussone provides much-needed tech support for national Bible translators in Mozambique and Southern Africa.

"My role in Bible translation is helping the local church and the language groups with IT issues," he says. "I'm also involved in training them how to use technology [as they] translate Scripture and share their work. I'm so thankful God gave me this opportunity to be part of Bible translation and blessed me with knowledge I can use to help the translators."

Today's Prayer: Dear Lord Jesus, thank You for giving Tomussone the ability to assist Bible translators! Thank you, Jesus, for the abilities You have given me. Please help me find new ways to serve You. In Jesus's name I pray. Amen.

Day 91: God Protected Them All

Daily Scripture Reading: Philippians 4:4–7

Do not be anxious about anything, but in every situation, by prayer and petition, with thanksgiving, present your requests to God. And the peace of God, which transcends all understanding, will guard your hearts and your minds in Christ Jesus. (verses 6–7)

TRANSLATORS ATTENDING A BIBLE TRANSLATION workshop during the pandemic diligently followed health guidelines and asked for prayer to keep Bible translation moving forward.

Bible translators in the city of Lome, Togo, in West Africa, would not be deterred. Despite potential risks associated with the coronavirus, thirty-eight eager national Bible translators, representing four different languages, convened for a Bible Translation workshop.

"Here in Togo, so far the situation is not serious," says Pastor Boureima. "We take all the precautions by following the established protection rules by [the] Togo COVID-19 Sanitary Office."

Donning masks, making regular use of available hand soap, and adhering to other strict health guidelines, the Bible translation teams dove into their work.

By the end, the Waci language group had translated twenty-five out of twenty-seven New Testament books. And the Wudu team finished an entire first draft of their

New Testament. These Bible translators had worked in the stress and fear of the unknown pandemic, yet God had protected them, and all of the translators returned home healthy. Praise God!

Today's Prayer: Oh Lord God, Your Word says not to be anxious and to pray in all circumstances. Thank you for protecting these Bible translators. Please help me to pray and trust You to be with us through the very difficult circumstances that come our way. I pray in Jesus's name. Amen.

Day 92: The Deaf Are Translating Scripture Too!

Daily Scripture Reading: Psalm 119:97–105

Your word is a lamp for my feet, a light on my path. (verse 105)

ATTENDING THE DEAF OWNED BIBLE TRANSLATION (DOT) workshop in Lesotho, Africa, were twelve Deaf Bible translators. All were qualified to translate in the Lesotho Sign Language, and they produced excellent work. For several of the translators, the more they pondered the Scriptures they read, the more they realized they were not following Jesus Christ.

During the intensive New Testament translation process and the filming of their sign language, six of the participants knew that God was calling them to Himself. By the end of the workshop, each of them made decisions to follow Jesus.

Just two months later, in a nearby country of Namibia, seven Deaf Bible translators met at a Deaf center for their DOT Bible Translation training. Part of their training was filming and editing videos in order to produce the Bible in their signed heart language.

The Deaf translators worked well together and completed seven chapters of the Gospel of Mark in the Namibia Sign language. Now that they have received training, they will continue to translate Scripture into their heart language following the workshop. The Lord had protected this small team of Bible translators and leaders from the coronavirus in the early days of the pandemic. Everyone returned to their home in safety and in good health. Praise God!

Eventually countries began to reopen for travel. Several sign language teams are completing their New Testament videos, and some Deaf teams are moving on to translate the Old Testament.

Today's Prayer: Thank you, Heavenly Father, for Your Word. And thank you that the Deaf can get Your Word in their own sign language. I pray that many deaf people will follow You. May we read, meditate, and obey Your Word today. Amen.

Day 93: "I gave my life to Him."

Daily Scripture Reading: John 8:25–32

Jesus said, "If you hold to my teaching, you are really my disciples. Then you will know the truth, and the truth will set you free." (verses 31–32)

"I WAS CAPTURED IN THE MIDDLE OF THE TOWN BY THE local police," says Tefera, recalling a terrifying day when he was fourteen years old, visiting his grandmother in her village in Ethiopia. "I didn't know what was going on, but they took me to prison."

Once in the prison, Tefera discovered that other family members had been arrested. Why? Because they had welcomed Christian missionaries into their home.

"On the nineteenth day of my imprisonment, they came and they beat us," Tefera says. "They tortured my uncle, and they tortured me. I was very angry and complained to God. I said, 'God, if you are true, you should make justice.'"

That night Tefera had a vivid dream. Someone kept calling to him and repeating, "God is alive.... He is here." When he awoke, Tefera told his uncle about the dream. His uncle listened closely and, moved by the dream, told Tefera, "You'll be free tomorrow."

The next day officials showed up and released Tefera. "On that day," Tefera remembers, "I knelt down, and I gave my life to Him."

Young Tefera made his way to the prime minister's office to seek help for his family. At first he was rebuffed because of his young age, but he kept pushing and speaking out about the injustice that his family was enduring. Finally, the regional president ordered the release of all of Tefera's family members.

Tefera is now a vital, influential leader in Bible translation. Not only did he experience God's faithfulness in those difficult days, but he also has seen how God's translated Word transforms hearts and lives.

Today's Prayer: Merciful God, thank you for the truth in Jesus Christ that sets us free. In Jesus's name. Amen.

Day 94: "God entrusted part of His great work on earth to us."

Daily Scripture Reading: John 15:1–17

I chose you and appointed you so that you might go and bear fruit—fruit that will last—and so that whatever you ask in my name the Father will give you. This is my command: Love each other. (verses 16–17)

YES, IT'S A MILESTONE! WE ARE CELEBRATING THE completion of the five hundredth New Testament translation supported by Wycliffe Associates with your help. Local churches were trained, resourced, and supported by Wycliffe Associates! This five hundredth New Testament was translated by and for the Northern Udmurt language group in Russia. Below, Linara shares her appreciation for being invited to become a Bible translator:

"I sincerely thank God for giving us the opportunity to translate the Bible into our own language," Linara says. "We feel very privileged and honored because of that. Bible translation work is a very exciting and humbling thing to do. It was fabulous to realize that God entrusted part of His great work on earth to us.

"Now I see how important it is to bring God's Word in people's own language. And I believe that through this translation of ours, many Udmurts will join us next to our Lord, and His Truth will make them all free of sin and death. Thank you for the opportunity you gave me to become part of God's plan."

Today's Prayer: Gracious Lord, thank you for Your work in the Udmurt community. Now they have the New Testament, which they can read at home and at church. Thank you, Lord, for leading your churches to complete these five hundred New Testament translations—and those since! Thank you for giving us all the opportunity to become a part of your plan. In Jesus's name I pray. Amen.

Day 95: "I was a beggar."

Daily Scripture Reading: John 6:30–40

Then Jesus declared, "I am the bread of life. Whoever comes to me will never go hungry, and whoever believes in me will never be thirsty." (verse 35)

NOT LONG AGO, SARA* WAS HAVING A HARD TIME making it from one day to the next. She would go from house to house asking for food. Sara was a beggar, a member of a nomadic tribe and considered "untouchable." One day a ministry partner met her on the street. Sara was invited to the ministry center and given a good meal.

Invited to come for a meal every day, she heard more and more about God's love, and her faith began to grow.

Today, Sara is a member of a Church Owned Bible Translation team. They're making great progress translating the New Testament into Lad,* Sara's heart language. She's leading the oral translation for her people.

"I thank God for choosing me to do this divine job," she says. "I was a beggar, but God is using me to give the Bread of Life to our own people. I will help give His Word in the Lad language not only to this present generation but to generations to come. This is a huge blessing!"

Today's Prayer: Father God, thank you for ministry partners that shared food and the Word with Sara. Please help me to clearly see people whose needs I can meet so they, in turn, will meet You and Your plan for their lives. I pray in the name of Jesus. Amen.

Names changed for security reasons.

Day 96: "I have seen hearts fill with joy."

Daily Scripture Reading: 2 Timothy 3:10–17

All Scripture is God-breathed and is useful for teaching, rebuking, correcting and training in righteousness, so that the servant of God may be thoroughly equipped for every good work. (verses 16–17)

ROGER* IS INTEGRAL TO BIBLE TRANSLATION PROJ-ects all across South Asia. His role is to help equip the local church and language communities.

Wycliffe Associates: "How did you get involved in Bible translation?"

Roger: "I started serving as a language surveyor in my home country, traveling to different places and gathering basic information like the population, the vitality of the language, the main religion, and whether there were believers in the community. This paved a way to find out if there [was] a need for Bible translation in the communities."

Wycliffe Associates: "Why is it important for people to have God's Word in their mother tongue?"

Roger: "2 Timothy 3:16 says, 'All Scripture is God-breathed and is useful for teaching, rebuking, correcting and training in righteousness. . . .' But what about those who don't have the Scriptures in their language? How will they know? To understand what God is communicating [to] us, we need the Bible in our mother tongue."

Wycliffe Associates: "How is Bible translation impacting lives in South Asia?"

Roger: "Wycliffe Associates is giving ownership of Bible translation to the local church by training, equipping, and empowering them. At the translation workshops, I have seen hearts fill with joy, as that work will significantly impact lives for generations."

Today's Prayer: Precious Lord, I pray that You will continue to use Roger in the work of Bible translation. I am blessed in doing the work You've prepared for me. Thank you, Lord Jesus, for loving us and using us in Your work around the world. Amen.

Name changed for security reasons.

Day 97: Brothers from Thousands of Miles Away

Daily Scripture Reading: Matthew 12:46–50

"For whoever does the will of my Father in heaven is my brother and sister and mother." (verse 50)

A BIBLE TRANSLATION TRAINER LED A BIBLE TRANSlation workshop in a nearby country and shared this report:

"A man came up to me and struggled to speak English. He thought about every sentence before he said it. He asked me, 'Do you have any brothers and sisters?' I told him how many brothers and sisters I had.

"I said, 'Do you have any brothers and sisters?'

"He said, 'I have four. But they have disowned me. Because I come to Christ, they don't want me for a brother.'

"I asked him, 'How large is your family?'

"He said, 'One. Mother, father dead. Brothers disown.'" And then he said, 'One family, Jesus. One brother, one father, one family. As long as I have Him, I am never alone.'

"He was one of the most passionate worshipers in the worship sessions. Then I realized why: Jesus is all he has, his only family left.

"I said to him, 'The one thing you can know in your heart is that you've chosen the brother who will never leave you. Your other brothers will turn against you, your parents will die, your friends. These friends here, you could be separated and never see each other again. You will always have the Lord with you.

"In that moment, we were brothers from thousands of miles away."

Today's Prayer: Father God, thank you that Jesus is with me and never will leave. In His name I pray. Amen.

Day 98: "If you believe Jesus, you will be saved."

> **Daily Scripture Reading:** Acts 16:22–36
>
> *He then brought them out and asked, "Sirs, what must I do to be saved?" They replied, "Believe in the Lord Jesus, and you will be saved." (verses 30–31)*

D R. Y,* A CHRISTIAN LEADER IN ASIA, SHARED THIS story with us about a Muslim imam who became a believer and shared the gospel with his neighbors.

The former imam's strategy was this: he opened the door of his house and let all his neighbors come in, and then he served them coffee or tea. He had written John 3:16 on the walls and on the ceiling of his home.

Dr. Y said, "When the people [came] to his house, he would say, 'Hey, good morning!' After he served them coffee or tea, he talked to them. 'Would you like to get salvation?'

"The people [answered], 'Yes, we would like to get salvation.'

"Then he told the people, 'Okay, please read [what] I already wrote on the wall, and please look on the ceiling . . .[and] over there.'

"When the people read this verse, he asked the question, 'It's very simple. Would you like to believe Jesus? If you believe Jesus, you will be saved. . . .' Even though he had been an imam, his house became a house church. There are more than 250 new believers in that place."

Dr. Y concluded, "This is the impact of the Bible translation. He . . . wrote on the wall and the ceiling, and the people came to Christ." Dr. Y also said that this group of believers have helped more than three thousand new Christian believers from Muslim backgrounds.

Today's Prayer: Dear Lord Jesus, You are indeed at work in the world, even using Bible translation and Scripture written on house walls! I praise You, Lord. Amen.

Name changed for security reasons.

Day 99: A Passion for Her People

Daily Scripture Reading: Psalm 40:9–11

I do not hide your righteousness in my heart; I speak of your faithfulness and your saving help. (verse 10)

ANNA* SPENT HER CHILDHOOD SUFFERING. BOTH of her parents died, so she was sent to live with an aunt and uncle. Even though they took great care of young Anna, she contracted an illness that would not leave her young body.

Her new family tried to find medical help and spent lots of money with doctor after doctor, but there was no help. Being Hindu, they followed all the prescribed rituals to appease the gods. But that was no help. They were certain Anna soon would die.

A distant relative asked if she could take Anna to her Christian church. Anna's family finally gave in because they felt they had no other choice. So, she was taken to a church where the Christians prayed over her. Anna thought this was no more help than her own religion.

But a few days later, Anna felt a little bit better. Then, in a few weeks' time, Anna realized she felt good. She felt really good. The Lord had answered the prayers of the Christian church. God had completely healed Anna!

Anna, with gratitude in her heart, returned to the church and learned about Jesus.

Now a young woman, Anna has a passion for her people in South Asia. She knows the local religions are meaningless. She is an integral part of the Rau* Bible translation team, and she even trains others to become Bible translators for their heart languages.

Today's Prayer: Oh God, You are faithful, and Anna has responded by sharing her faith as a Bible translator. Thank you for your faithfulness! Amen.

*Names changed for security reasons.

Day 100: "It's our duty."

Daily Scripture Reading: Colossians 3:18–25

Whatever you do, work at it with all your heart, as working for the Lord, not for human masters, since you know that you will receive an inheritance from the Lord as a reward. (verses 23–24)

THE FOLLOWING IS AN INTERVIEW WITH NAOMI,* A national Bible translator:

Wycliffe Associates: "How did God lead you to be involved in Bible translation?"

Naomi: "My mother was participating in a Wycliffe Associates translation workshop for the Bee* Bible (my heart language). I only went to keep her company."

Wycliffe Associates: "How did you become a Bible translation training facilitator?"

Naomi: "I was so encouraged when we completed the Bee New Testament, and I started to get involved in other translation events, encouraging others through my experience. I soon realized that God was leading me into this and was using me for His kingdom."

Wycliffe Associates: "Why do you feel it's important for people to have God's Word in their mother tongue?"

Naomi: "When people read the Bible in their own language, it's easier for them to understand.... The message goes deeper into their hearts."

Wycliffe Associates: "Is there anything on your heart that you'd like to share with people who support this ministry?"

Naomi: "I would love to thank all the generous partners. If it wasn't for their help and support, this great work would not be possible. God has placed us in different locations, but it is our duty, working together, to bring the translated gospel to all people."

Today's Prayer: Faithful God, You have placed each one of Your children in different places and given us each work to do. Help me honor You in my work today. In Jesus's name. Amen.

Names changed for security reasons.

Day 101: Remembering Them in Prayer

Daily Scripture Reading: Ephesians 1:15–23

I have not stopped giving thanks for you, remembering you in my prayers. (verse 16)

PRAY YOU WILL BE BLESSED, AS I WAS, READING THIS email from a dear prayer partner in Uganda as he encouraged all Wycliffe Associates prayer warriors:

"Praise the Lord for His mercy and for enabling each one of us in their respective capacity. For the prayer warriors, I want to tell [you] that in all the work that is being done in [Bible] translation and within Wycliffe Associates, it's our responsibility to pray and intercede for the entire [ministry]. I want to call upon [you] again to not stop, because we are still needed, and the work of [Bible] translation is still here to stay until the world is filled with the gospel. Through this we are also taking part in the Great Commission in Matthew 28:19.

"So, as we intercede for Wycliffe Associates, the Word of God is being preached. Let's go deeper and deeper in praying, fasting, and interceding.

"I thank God for the way I have been in some of the community checking. I was amazed when the congregation heard the Word of God for the first time in their own mother tongue. Their New Testament is almost done now.... And they also want the Old Testament. When I heard such, I praised the Lord and glorified the Name of Jesus." –Deus Ngabirano, Uganda.

Today's Prayer: Dear Lord, may we indeed go deeper in praying, fasting, and interceding for those hearing Your Word in their heart language. We pray together for Bible translation in the great name of Jesus. Amen.

Day 102: Living Water for the Soul and Clean Water for the Body

Daily Scripture Reading: John 7:37–41

Whoever believes in me, as Scripture has said, rivers of living water will flow from within them. By this he meant the Spirit, whom those who believed in him were later to receive. Up to that time the Spirit had not been given since Jesus had not yet been glorified. On hearing his words, some of the people said, "Surely this man is the Prophet." Others said, "He is the Messiah." (verses 38–41)

N TOGO, AFRICA, THE ANA LANGUAGE GROUP HEADS out each morning with buckets and jugs to get water for the day. They are so thankful for the water system that, through partners like you, the Wycliffe Associates Community Development team installed to help provide clean water.

And this community is getting more than clean water! Bible translators are providing newly translated Scripture for the local pastors, who are taking turns reading at the well as containers are being filled with clean water. The Ana people are so inspired that they share the water and God's Word freely with their Muslim neighbors.

North and west of Togo is a country called Guinea. In this country, the Soussous people could only get water from a contaminated river that causes dysentery, cholera, and typhoid fever. That is, until a clean water project was launched by

Wycliffe Associates to serve local Bible translators and their communities.

Pastor Daniel says, "God will enable us to announce the gospel to the people. Thank you again for this achievement. Thank you to those who gave. May the Lord shower His blessing on you!"

Today's Prayer: How we praise You, Lord, for these communities, and many more around the world, that are sharing the Living Water for the soul right along with clean water for the body. In Jesus's name. Amen.

Day 103: They Had Been Bullied Before

Daily Scripture Reading: Matthew 5:43–48

You have heard that it was said, "Love your neighbor and hate your enemy." But I tell you, love your enemies and pray for those who persecute you, that you may be children of your Father in heaven. He causes his sun to rise on the evil and the good and sends rain on the righteous and the unrighteous. (verses 43-45)

AIDA LOVES JESUS. SHE IS A WIFE, A MOTHER TO SIX children, and a grandmother living in the Philippines. And she is a dedicated Bible translator. Until recently, her people, the B'lann Fungol, were considered *less than* by their neighbor communities. They were belittled because their language was different.

"We have been bullied before because we are different, and we speak differently," Aida says. "But because of this ministry, I have refreshed my love for our language. And I've learned not to be ashamed of our language, that it is a gift from the Lord."

Aida has been blessed by the Scriptures she is translating. And her faith and love for God have grown. "My knowledge of the Bible, as well as my spiritual journey with the Lord, has been refreshed as well," she says.

The B'lann Fungol translation team, including Aida, have finished their New Testament in their heart language. Praise God!

Today's Prayer: Oh Lord, life can be so difficult for the "underdog," and here You tell us to love our enemies and pray for them. Oh God, I pray You give the B'lann Fungo people opportunities to do good deeds for their bullying neighbors. And Lord, please help me to forgive and do good to those who make my life difficult. In the name of Your Son, Jesus. Amen.

Day 104: He Is Our Strength

Daily Scripture Reading: 2 Corinthians 12:5–10

But he said to me, "My grace is sufficient for you, for my power is made perfect in weakness." Therefore I will boast all the more gladly about my weaknesses, so that Christ's power may rest on me. That is why, for Christ's sake, I delight in weaknesses, in insults, in hardships, in persecutions, in difficulties. For when I am weak, then I am strong. (verses 9–10)

PASTOR TIMOTHY VOLUNTEERS HIS TIME TO LEAD Church Owned Bible Translation training workshops. He is currently leading eight Zambian translation projects that are not even his own language. He is sold out to Bible translation's lifesaving impact!

One day Pastor Timothy climbed into the back seat of a taxi, just like he often does when heading home. The taxi went a short distance—and then suddenly stopped. Men jumped in, one on each side of Pastor Timothy. They beat him mercilessly, robbed him, and threw him out of the moving car.

The very next day, though bruised and battered, Pastor Timothy boarded a bus to travel fourteen hours to a village where he led a Bible translation workshop for two Zambian language groups. Pastor Timothy set the example of depending on God for his strength. That workshop resulted in the New Testament translations being completed for the Lamba and Mbunda people.

What an impact! Pastor Timothy is totally committed to bringing God's Word to the lost. He is seeing churches and communities receive God's Word where, not long ago, there never had been even one verse in their heart language.

Today's Prayer: Ever-giving God, thank you for giving Pastor Timothy the strength he needed to fulfill his commitment to Bible translation. Though our bodies are weak, thank you for being our strength. In Jesus's name. Amen.